Better

NEWS

FOR THE

HEBREWS

< A COMMENTARY ON HEBREWS >

WAYNE DUNAWAY

PREFACE

BETTER NEWS FOR THE HEBREWS: A Commentary on the Hebrews Emphasizing the Superior Blessing of the New Covenant.

Better News for the Hebrews is the result of years and years of Bible study. It was written and re-written over and over as knowledge increased and God helped me to what I hope is a "better" concept of the "better things" God has provided for us (Heb. 11:40). Obviously various ones have enlightened me on numerous passages and different concepts concerning Christianity and the sacrifice of Jesus as the years went by. Some of the things that I wrote in the earlier years had to be modified later and some things had to be eliminated altogether. Growth involves change and change is the result of growth—both in knowledge and wisdom as well as understanding. No one starts out or ends up knowing it all, but we do learn as we grow and grow as we learn. This is God's way of dealing with His children. He is patient, loving and kind toward us at all times as we learn to appreciate what He has done in providing these "better things" for us.

Better news? Better things for us! Who is "us"? What are the "better things"? The book of Hebrews answers both questions in detail. This is the better news for us in Hebrews. It was written to encourage Christians to remain faithful to Jesus. The writer goes to great lengths to describe how great Jesus and the salvation He has provided really is. "Better News for the Hebrews" points to things promised by God and provided by the coming of Jesus into the world to be our High Priest and sacrifice for sin. The book emphasizes the weakness of the Old Covenant and the strength of the New. The fact that Jesus is superior to the prophets, angels, Moses, Joshua, Aaron, and the Levitical priesthood is clearly taught throughout the book. Therefore He provides a superior cov-

enant, priesthood, and sacrifice for believers than were provided to those under the Old Covenant. These "better things"
results in "Better News." The book stresses how much better
it is for us than it was for the saints in previous ages. The
word "better" is used over and over again. That one word is
one of the best words to describe what it really means to be
a believer in Jesus. It is just "better." The book of Hebrews
magnifies the power of faith and what faith has done and will
do for believers of all ages. It exhorts us to encourage each
other and warns us against falling away from the faith. It
even relates how persecution and trials provide encouragement for us when viewed as God's training and discipline to
make us stronger and better. Everything in the book points
to the fact the God has "provided something better for us"
(Hebrews 11:40), or as the title of this book suggests, *Better
News for the Hebrews.*"

Actually I think of the words good, better, and best when I
think of God's dealing with man. God provided *good* things
for His people during the Old Covenant times (Rom. 7:12).
But He has provided some *better* things for us because of the
coming of Jesus (Heb. 11:40). And He will provide the *best*
things for believers of all ages in the "world to come" (Heb.
2:5). All of these points are emphasized in this great book of
the Bible.

Wayne Dunaway
November, 2017

TABLE OF CONTENTS

Section One: The Superior Person of Christ (Chapters 1:1-4:13)

Hebrews 1 — Jesus is Superior to the Prophets and Angels
Hebrews 2 – Jesus Provides a Superior Salvation
Hebrews 3 – Jesus is Superior to Moses
Hebrews 4 – Jesus is Superior to Joshua

Section Two: The Superior Priesthood of Christ (Chapters 4:14-10:39)

Hebrews 5 – Jesus is Superior to Aaron
Hebrews 6 – Jesus Offers Superior Hope for Christians
Hebrews 7 – Jesus is Superior to the Levitical Priesthood
Hebrews 8 – Jesus is the Mediator of a Superior Covenant
Henrews 9 – Jesus Ministers in a Superior Tabernacle
Hebrews 10 – Jesus Offered a Superior Sacrifice

Section Three: The Superior Position of Those in Christ (Chapters 11:1-13:25)

Hebrews 11 – Jesus Provides Superior Blessings
Hebrews 12 – Jesus is a Superior Source of Encouragement
Hebrews 13 – Jesus Establishes a Superior Relationship

Appendix #1 – The World to Come
Appendix #2 – The Security of the Believer
Appendix #3 – Forsaking the Assembly

INTRODUCTION TO THE BOOK OF HEBREWS

*(The title of the book is not inspired,
but was added by translators)*

I. TO WHOM WAS THE BOOK WRITTEN?

The book was written to Hebrew Christians.

1. They were holy brethren (Heb. 3:1).
2. They had been enlightened (Heb. 10:32).
3. They were Christians who could pray (Heb. 13:18).
4. They were good Christians in many respects (Heb. 10:32-34).
5. They were not new converts (Heb. 5:12).
6. They were Jewish Christians probably living in and around Jerusalem.

II. THE BOOK WRITTEN FOR THE BENEFIT OF ALL

The book, while addressed to the Hebrews, was written for all Christians.

1. What Jesus said to apostles, He said to all (Mark 13:17).
2. The letter Paul wrote to Titus was for the benefit of all (Titus 1:4; 3:15).
3. All epistles were written for all to read and observe (Col. 4:16; 1 Thess. 5:27).
4. What Jesus said to the church in Ephesus was for all to hear (Rev. 2:1, 7).
5. The above references are enough to show that Hebrews (as well as all of the books of the New Testament) was written for the benefit of all Christians.

III. THE THEME OF THE BOOK

The theme of the book is "the superiority of Christianity over Judaism" or the superiority of the New Covenant over the Old Covenant or as I would say it, *The Superiority of the Lord's Authority.*

A. Hebrews deals with the Lord's authority over the devil and death.

> 1. Jesus destroyed him who had the power of death (Heb. 2:9).
> 2. The devil's power is limited to God's sovereign control, but Jesus still defeated the main power that the devil had by His death on the cross.

B. The book deals with the Lord's authority over the Law of Moses.

> 1. He took away the old covenant in order to establish the new (Heb. 10:9).
> 2. He replaced the first covenant with the second. (Hebrews 8:6-12).

C. The book also deals with the Lord's authority over sin and temptation.

> 1. He helps those who are tempted (Heb. 2:14-18).
> 2. There is always grace to help in time of need (Heb. 4:14-16).

IV. AN OUTLINE OF THE BOOK

A. The Superior PERSON of Christ (Chapters 1:1-4:13).

> 1. Jesus is superior to the prophets (1:1-3).
> 2. Jesus is superior to the angels (1:4-2:18).
> 3. Jesus is superior to Moses (3:1-19).

4. Jesus is superior to Joshua (4:1-13).

B. The Superior PRIESTHOOD of Christ (Chapters 4:14-10:39).

    1. Jesus is a superior High Priest (5:1-7:28).
    2. Jesus has a superior covenant (8:1-9:22).
    3. Jesus offered a superior sacrifice (9:23-10:39).

C. The Superior POSITION of those in Christ (Chapters 11:1-13:25).

    1. Jesus supplies superior blessings (11:1-40).
    2. Jesus is a superior source of encouragement 12:1-28).
    3. Jesus establishes a superior relationship (13:1-25).

V. WHY WAS THE BOOK WRITTEN?

The book was written to warn about falling away from Christ. It was written to discourage these Jewish Christians from leaving Christ and the gospel and returning to Judaism and/or legalism. It was written to encourage them to remain faithful to Christ.

A. This explains the many warnings against apostasy.

    1. They are warned against neglecting so great a salvation (Heb. 2:3-4).
    2. They are warned against departing from the living God (Heb. 3:12).
    3. They are warned against falling away (Heb. 6:1-6).
    4. They are warned against forsaking the assembly and sinning willfully (Heb. 10:25-31).
    5. They are warned against turning away from Him who speaks from heaven (Heb. 12:25).

B. This also explains the statements about "better" things of Christianity.

    1. Better than angels (Heb. 1:4).
    2. Better High Priest (Heb. 7:7).
    3. Better hope (Heb. 7:19).
    4. Better testament (Heb. 7:22).
    5. Better Mediator (Heb. 8:6a).
    6. Better promises (Heb. 8:6b).
    7. Better sacrifices (Heb. 9:23).
    8. Better possession (Heb. 10:34).
    9. Better country (Heb. 11:16).
    10. Better resurrection (Heb. 11:35).
    11. Better things for us (Heb. 11:40).
    12. Better bloodshed (Heb. 12:24).

The book can be summarized in one verse:

God having provided something better for us that they should not be made perfect apart from us **(Hebrews 11:40). Or as the book title suggests, "Better News for the Hebrews."**

SECTION ONE:

THE SUPERIOR PERSON
OF CHRIST
(Chapters 1:1-4:13)

HEBREWS
Chapter One

JESUS IS SUPERIOR TO THE PROPHETS
AND ANGELS

Special Note: In this first chapter the Hebrew writer will show that Jesus Christ is the complete and final revelation of God to man. He will prove that Jesus has a greater message and that He is a greater Messenger. Therefore *He is superior to the prophets and the Angels.*

JESUS IS SUPERIOR TO THE PROPHETS (Heb. 1:1-3).

Verse 1: God, who at various times - **That is, many times or many parts.**

1. **God revealed His will in many parts on many occasions little by little.**
2. **The Bible was not dropped out of heaven all at once, completely finished.**
3. **God used about 40 different men over a period of over 1500 years to finish His complete revelation.**
4. **For example, the prophecies concerning Christ were revealed little by little. (See Gen. 3:15; 12:1-3; 49:10; Deut. 18:15-18; Isaiah 7:14; Isa. 9:6-7; Isa. 53; etc.)**

and in various ways - **Different ways or methods.**

1. **This refers to the different ways the prophets made known the revelations to the fathers.**
2. **Inspired songs, poetry, narrative, object lessons, etc.**
3. **Types, figures, dark sayings, as well as plain language, were all used by the prophets in revealing the message of God.**

spoke in time past to the fathers by the prophets - A prophet is one who speaks for another. This refers to the prophets in the Old Testament and includes the heads of the family in the Patriarchal Age.

Verse 2: has in these last days - The "last days" refers to the Christian Age, which was and is the last dispensation of time on earth. In the beginning there was the Patriarchal Age which lasted about 2500 years, next was the Mosaic Age which lasted about 1500 years; and then finally there was the last age or the Christian Age which began in Acts 2 and ends on this earth when Jesus returns the second time (Heb. 9:28). The "last days" will ultimately give way to the "world to come" which is the eternal age in the new heaven and new earth.

1. Acts 2:15-17 - Spirit was to be poured out in the last days.
2. Luke 24:46-47 - Authority of Jesus over the church on earth began in Acts 2 and will end at His second coming.
3. Acts 11:15 - Peter referred to this as the "beginning."
4. Other views:
    a. Closing period of the Jewish Age.
    b. Ministry of Christ and Apostles.
    c. Started Christ's earthly ministry and ends at the second coming.
5. Matt. 28:18-20 - The "last days" are the days in which Jesus speaks to us as the next statement clearly indicates. The words of Jesus are to be taught until the end of the age which will occur when He comes the second time.

spoken to us by His Son - Jesus spoke the words that the Father gave Him to speak.

1. John 14:10 – "The words I speak, I speak not of myself...."
2. John 8:28 - As the Father taught, He spoke.
3. John 3:34 - Jesus spoke the words of God.
4. John 12:49 - The Father gave Him commandment what to say.
5. Matt. 28:18 – Jesus has the authority to speak.

whom He has appointed heir of all things, - An heir is one who inherits what the Father has.

1. Col. 1:16 - All things were made by Him and "for Him."
2, Heb. 2:10 – By Him are all things and "for whom" are all things.
3. Rom. 8:17 - An interesting side note is that Christians are joint heirs with Christ.
4. Rom. 4:13 – Abraham is "heir of the world" and so are all believers who have the faith of our father Abraham (Rom. 4:16).

through whom also He made the worlds - Jesus was the active agent in creation. All things made by the "Word" (John 1:1-3, 14).

1. Col. 1:16 - By Christ were all things created.
2. Eph. 3:9 - God created all things by Jesus Christ.
3. Gen. 1:26 - "Let us...make man in our image..." The word "us" and "our" proves that more than one member of the Godhead was in on creation.

Verse 3: *who being the brightness of His glory and the express image of His person* - All that God is has been expressed in Christ.

1. John 14:8-9 - "He that hath seen me hath seen the Father."
2. John 1:18 - "No man has seen God; the Son has declared him."

NOTE - When we see Christ, we see the Father. His attitude and behavior when He was on earth is the same as the Father's would have been if He had come to earth instead of Christ. The way Christ acted in time of trouble, temptation, etc. is the same identical way the Father would have acted. The way He treated others is exactly as the Father would/does treat others.

and upholding all things by the word of His power **- Christ not only created the world but He keeps the world going.**

when He had by Himself purged our sins **- He took away our sins. He cleansed us from our sins by His death.**

1.   John 1:29 - Takes away sin.
2.   Matt. 1:21 - He saves from sin.

sat down at the right hand of the Majesty on high, **- He sat down on the right hand of God.**

1.   Acts 2:33 - Peter said that is where He is.
2.   Heb. 8:1 - He is on the right hand of Majesty in the heaven.
3.   Heb. 12:2 - He is on the right hand of the throne of God.

CONCLUSION: Why is Jesus superior to the prophets? Because:

1.   He is the *Son* (v.2a).
2.   He is *heir* of all things (v.2b).
3.   He *made the worlds* (v.2c).
4.   He is the *express image* of God (v.3a).
5.   He *upholds all things* by the word of His power (v. 3b).
6.   He is *seated at the right hand* of God (v.3c).

7.   He is more than just a *prophet*. He is also Priest and
      King.
      a.   *Prophet* - He spoke (v.1).
      b.   *Priest* - He made purification for sins (v.2a).
      c.   *King* - He sat down on the throne (v.2b).
8. Christ is superior to the prophets because these things
   cannot be said about the prophets, but they can be said
   about the Son.

JESUS IS SUPERIOR TO THE ANGELS (Heb. 1:4-14)

Special Note: Not only does he prove that Jesus is superior to
the OT prophets, *He is also superior to the angels.*

Verse 4: *having become so much better than the angels* - Jesus
is better than the angels. The following statements will tell
why and how He is better.

   1. Gal. 3:19 - Angels were in on giving the law.
   2. Gen. 3:24 - They guarded the way to the tree of life.
   3. Gen. 18-19 - They appeared to Abraham and Lot.
   4. They made numerous appearances in the Old Testa-
       ment. The Jews thought angels were "it." Angels were
       second only to God Himself.

*as He has by inheritance obtained a more excellent name than
they* - The more excellent name is "Son." This is the first reason Christ is better than the angels.

   1. Men and angels are referred to as sons of God.
       a. Gen. 6:2 - The descendants of Seth called sons of
           God.
       b. Job 1:6 - Angels called sons of God.
       c. 1 John 3:1 - Christians called sons of God.
   2. What is so special then about the name Son?
       a. Jesus is not *a* son, but *the* Son.
       a. Men and angels are called sons because they are
          created and adopted as sons, but Christ is a Son

by inheritance. Christ inherited the name Son.

3. **He is a Son in a sense that no other being in heaven or on earth is.**

Verse 5: *For to which of the angels did He ever say: "You are My Son, Today I have begotten You"?* **- This is quoted from Psalms 2:7. When was this said of Christ? There are two possible answers: (1) At His birth into the world; (2) At His resurrection. This statement probably refers primarily to His resurrection, but that would not be possible without His birth.**

And again: "I will be to Him a Father, And He shall be to Me a Son"? **- This is a quotation from 2 Samuel 7:14.**

1. **Acts 13:33-34 - Paul connects Psalm 2:7 with the resurrection.**
2. **Romans 1:4 - By His resurrection Jesus is declared to be the Son of God with power. Thus Christ was produced from the grave rather than produced as a child in a normal sense. His being begotten from the grave is primarily referred to here. This was not said of angels.**

Verse 6*: but when He again brings the firstborn into the world* **- This statement probably refers to His resurrection made possible by His birth.**

He says: "Let all the angels of God worship Him." **- This shows that Christ is Deity (Divine Being) and worthy to be worshipped by angels. Angels "worship" the Son which again shows the Son is superior to angels.**

Verse 7*: And of the angels He says: "Who makes His angels spirits* **- They are servants. They serve and do service.**

1. **Heb. 1:14 - They minister. They are ministering Spirits.**
2. **Rev. 1:20 – Likely there are angels who watch over the local churches.**

And His ministers a flame of fire." - They are called a flame of fire because they sometimes take on the appearance of fire.

1. 2 Kings 2:11 - Angels as "fire" appear to Elijah.
2. 2 Kings 6:15-17 - The "horses and chariots of fire" were, no doubt, angels. Their appearance was like horses and chariots of fire.

Verse 8*: But to the Son He says: "Your throne, O God, is forever and ever* - The Son is here called "God." He is not "God the Father," but He is "God the Son." He is Deity. He is one who possesses Divine nature. He is a Supreme Being. He is God.

1. John 1:1 - The "Word" was God.
2. Acts 20:28 - Here Christ is called God.
3. John 20:28 - Here Christ is called God.

A scepter - A ruler's staff. A rod held in the hands of kings as a token of authority. Christ has a throne and a ruler's staff which shows that He is already a King now.

of righteousness is the scepter of Your kingdom" - This refers to the fact that Christ rules right and does right.

1. 1 John 2:1 - He is Jesus Christ the righteous.
2. 2 Tim. 4:8 - He is a Righteous Judge.
3. Isaiah 53:11 – He is a "righteous Servant."

Verse 9*: You have loved righteousness* - This refers to the fact that Jesus loved right and therefore He loved doing right.

1. Matt. 3:15 - He was baptized to "fulfill all righteouness."
2. John 6:38 - He proved He loved right because He obeyed the Father.
3. Heb. 4:15 - He was without sin which proved He

loved doing right.

and hated lawlessness - That is, He hated wrong. Christ loved right and hated wrong.

1. Ps. 119:104 - Those who understand God's word hate every false way.
2. Matt. 21:12 - His cleansing the temple proved that He hated wrong.

Therefore God, Your God - God the Father is the God of Jesus. In Matthew 27:46 Jesus prayed to the Father, "My God, My God...

has anointed You With the oil of gladness more than Your companions - This might refer to the Holy Spirit.

1. Acts 10:38 - Christ was anointed with the power of the Spirit.
2. John 3:34; Lk. 4:1 - Christ received the indwelling Spirit.

Verse 10: *And: "You, Lord, in the beginning laid the foundation of the earth, and the heavens are the work of Your hands.* - This verse is a quotation from Ps. 102:25. This verse refers to Christ the Son.

1. John 1:1-3; Col. 1:16; Heb. 1:1-2 - He laid the foundation of the earth, and the heavens are works of His hands.
2. Eph. 3:9 – God created all things by Jesus Christ.

 Verse 11: *They will perish* - That is, the heaven and earth that were created in the beginning will perish.

1. Matt. 24:35 - Heaven and earth shall pass away.
2. 2 Peter 3:10 – The heavens shall pass away with great noise and earth shall be burned up.

3. 2 Peter 3:13 – There will be a "new heaven and new earth" at His coming.

but You remain; And they will all grow old like a garment - That is, Jesus shall remain. Christ will continue, but the earth will finish its course and be destroyed.

1. Ps. 90:2 - Because He is God, He is "from everlasting to everlasting."
2. Heb. 13:8 - He abides forever.
3. Micah 5:2 - His going forth has been "from everlasting."
4. Heb. 1:12 - His years shall not fail.

Verse 12: *Like a cloak You will fold them up, And they will be changed. But You are the same, And Your years will not fail -* Christ is powerful enough to roll up the earth as easily as a man would fold up his clothes or coat. And one day He will do just that, but He Himself will always continue.

Verse 13: *But to which of the angels has He ever said: -* This was never said to any angel.

Sit at My right hand - This is a quotation from Ps. 110:1 and it applies to Christ. Peter applied it to Christ in the first sermon (Acts 2:34-35).

Till I make Your enemies Your footstool"? - It was the custom of kings to walk on their enemies necks as a token of their complete victory over them. Enemies were used as footstools.

1. 1 Cor. 15:24-27 - Christ will reign on this earth until the last enemy is destroyed.
2. Rev. 20:10-15 - All His enemies will be subdued by Him including the devil and death.

Verse 14: *Are they not all ministering spirits sent forth to min-*

ister for those who will inherit salvation? - The angels serve those whom Christ saves. God has used angels all along to carry out His work. Some New Testament examples are:

1. Lk. 1:11-13 - Angels announced the birth of John.
2. Lk. 1:26-36 - Angels announced the birth of Jesus.
3. Matt. 4:11 - Angels ministered to Christ after temption.
4. Luke 22:43 - Angels strengthened Jesus in the garden.
5. Acts 8:26 - Angel spoke to Phillip.
6. Acts 10:7 - Angel appeared to Cornelius.
7. Acts 27:23 - Angel comforted Paul on a ship.
8. Acts 5:19 - Angel released Peter and John from prison. (See also Acts 12:7)
9. Acts 12:23 - Angel killed Herod.

Question: Do angels minister to us today? I'm sure that they do. They may or may not minister in miraculous appearances as they have in times past, but they do minister in various ways. God has and does employ angels to minister for the saints (Heb. 1:14). What might they do for us?

1. Protect us (Ps. 91:11-12).
2. Deliver us (Ps. 34:7).
3. They can minister without being seen (2 Kings 6:17).
4. They may have custody of the souls of the righteous at death (Lk. 16:22).
5. They have power to take care of us if God wishes them to. One angel killed 185,000 men in one night (Isaiah 37:36).
6. They sometimes appear as humans (Gen. 18-19).
7. They are in charge of and watch over God's people (Dan. 12:1; Rev. 1:20).

CONCLUSION: How is the Son superior to angels? He is superior:

1. In name (v. 4).
2. In things said of him (v. 5).

3. In that angels worship him (v. 6).

4. In that angels are ministers while he is the Son
of God (vs. 7-8).

5. In that He has a throne and kingdom (v. 8).

6. In that He is God (v. 9).

7. In that He made the heavens and earth (v. 10).

8. In that He will bring an end to the world (v. 11-12)

9. In that He was told to sit on right hand (v. 13).

10. In that angels minister to those Jesus saves (v. 14).

NOTE - These things said of Jesus could not be said of angels.
Therefore, He is *superior to the angels*.

SPECIAL NOTE - Keep in mind that some of these Hebrew
Christians were about to return to Judaism. The Jews could
say: "Look, we have the temple, the sacrifices, the Priesthood,
and the Law of Moses and the things men can see." And they
could say, "You Christians don't have anything you can see."
The book was written to show the Hebrew Christians that
they had something far better than those in Judaism (Heb.
11:40). Every facet of the Christian system was superior to
that of Judaism as the remainder of the book will continue
to prove.

HEBREWS CHAPTER TWO

JESUS OFFERS A SUPERIOR SALVATION (Heb. 2:1-18)

Special Note: Since Jesus is superior to the prophets and better than the angels, He provides a *Superior Salvation* for those who believe (Heb. 2:1-18)

Verse 1: *Therefore we must give the more earnest heed to the things we have heard, lest we drift away* - The word "therefore" connects what is said here with what is said in the first chapter. Therefore - since Jesus is superior to the prophets and angels, and is Himself "God" - we need to give the more earnest heed to the things He has said; lest we let His words slip out of our minds and drift away from Christ.

Verse 2: *For if the word spoken through angels proved steadfast* - This refers to the Law of Moses. Angels had something to do with giving the Law of Moses, although it may not be clear exactly what it was.

    1. **Acts 7:53 - The Law was by the direction of angels.**
    2. **Gal. 3:19 - The Law of Moses was appointed through angels by the hand of a mediator.**

***and every transgression and disobedience received a just reward* - This means that those who transgressed the Law of Moses paid the penalty for violating that law. They did not escape. They were punished.**

    1. **Heb. 10:28 - Those who despised Moses' law died without mercy.**

2. **Num. 15:30-36 - Here a man is killed for presumptuously violating the Sabbath.**

Verse 3: *how shall we escape* **- If those who despised Moses' law were punished, how shall we escape if we neglect what the Lord Himself has said? The answer is that there is no escape!**

1. **2 Thess. 1:7-9 - Those who don't obey will be punished and there is no escape.**
2. **Heb. 10:26-29 - Those Christians who neglect to continue to do God's will shall not escape.**
3. **Heb. 12:25 – This verse answers that question directly…there is no escape!**

if we neglect **- This is exactly what many of the Hebrew Christians were about to do. They were about to neglect this great salvation.**

so great a salvation, which at the first began to be spoken by the Lord **- Why is the salvation so great?**

1. **Heb. 2:3 - It first began to be spoken by the Lord.**
2. **Heb. 2:3-4; Mk. 16:20 - It was confirmed by miracles. There can be no doubt about it being true.**
3. **It is great because of the many great things that are involved in it. For example, look at the great things in John 3:16:**

   a. **For God - God is the greatest being.**
   b. **So Loved - Love is the greatest thing.**
   c. **The World - The world is the greatest number.**
   d. **That He gave His only begotten Son - The Son is the greatest gift.**
   e. **That whoever believes in Him - Faith "in Him" is the greatest faith.**
   f. **Should   not perish - Perishing in hell is the greatest tragedy.**

     g.   But have everlasting life - Everlasting life is
           the greatest blessing.

and was confirmed to us by those who heard Him - This refers primarily to the apostles. Their words were confirmed
by miracles.

1.   Acts 1:8 - Apostles were His witnesses.
2.   1 John 1:1-3 - Apostles saw and heard Him.
3.   John 17:20 - Men believe on Jesus because of the
     apostles' word.

Verse 4: *God also bearing witness both with signs and wonders,
with various miracles, and gifts of the Holy Spirit, according to
His own will?* – The main purpose of the miracles, signs, and
wonders was to confirm the word.

1. Mk. 16:17-20 - The Lord worked with them and
   confirmed their word with the accompanying signs.
   (See also Acts 2:43; 5:12; 6:6, 8; 8:6).
2. 1 Cor. 12:8-10; Eph. 4:8,11; Mk. 16:17, 18 - These
   are the signs and gifts that were given.
3. Acts 8:18 - Miraculous spiritual gifts were
   generally given to others by the laying on of the
   apostles' hands. (See Acts 6:6; 19:6; Rom. 1:11;
   2 Tim. 1:6).
4. The gifts were given to confirm the word and
   when the word was revealed and confirmed, the
   miracles, signs, and wonders that confirmed the
   word ceased. This explains that, while God still
   does miracles and wonders when He pleases
   (Ps. 115:2), He is not doing the numerous amount
   of miracles that we read about in the book of Acts
   when the word was being revealed and confirmed.
      a. 1 Cor. 13:8-10 - Gifts that "confirmed the word"
      lasted until the perfect or complete revelation came.
      (See James 1:25).
      b. Eph. 4:8-11 - The miraculously gifted men were

to last until "the faith" was completely revealed and confirmed. That is, until everything God wanted us to know concerning the revelation of Christ was complete.

c. Micah 7:15 - Micah may suggest that the completed revelation and confirming the word would last about forty years.

d. Jude 1:3 - "The faith" has been once for all delivered and was revealed on Pentecost (Acts. 6:7). But the things we needed to know in order to have a better knowledge of Christ and His will for us took a while to reveal and be confirmed to the saints.

e. Philippians 1:27 - "The faith" is the faith of the gospel.

Verse 5: *For He has not put the world to come, of which we speak, in subjection to angels* - This means that the world to come was not going to be under the authority of angels, but under the authority of God and the Lamb (Rev. 22:3).

1. 2 Peter 3:15-16 says that some of the things Paul wrote are hard to be understood and Hebrews 2:5 proves that he was right, because it is hard to understand for some

2. What is the "world to come?"

   a. Some say it is the present Christian Age. The Law of Moses was ordained by angels (Gal. 3:19) but the "world to come" is under the sole authority of Christ.

   b. Looking at it from the Old Testament point of view, the Christian dispensation would have been the "world to come."

   c. Mk. 10:30 - Christ does have all authority now in the Christian age (Matt. 28:18). But there is still an "age to come."

   d. Heb. 5:6 - This verse refers to the "powers" of the "world to come." The phrase "world to come" indicates that there will be an age after this one and that believers experience the same kind of "power" now that we will experience then but likely not to the same degree now as then.

e. In my judgment, the "world to come" refers to life in the new heaven and new earth after the coming of Jesus.

f. The kingdom on this earth will translate into the everlasting state of the kingdom in the "new heaven and new earth" after this earth is destroyed (2 Pet. 3:8-13).

g. It is at the second coming of Jesus that believers will be granted an entrance into the "everlasting kingdom of our Lord and Savior Jesus Christ" (2 Pet. 1:13).

h. The ultimate fulfillment of this must be in the new heaven and new earth referred to in Isaiah 65:17; 2 Peter 3:13; and Revelation 21-22.

i. Eph. 1:21 – There is "this age" which is primarily the Christian age now and "that which is to come" which ultimately will be in the "new heaven and new earth." (2 Pet. 3:13; Rev. 21:1).

NOTE: See the Appendix #1 at the end of this book concerning the "World to Come."

Verse 6: *But one in a certain place testified, saying* - This refers to what David said in Psalm 8:3-8.

1. In verses 6-8, Paul quotes what David taught about man.

a. He shows that in God's order of creation, man is of a lower order than angels.

b. His bringing this up sets the stage for the rest of this chapter.

2. In the remainder of this chapter, Paul shows that Christ became a man (not an angel) in order to redeem man from sin and restore his proper place in the "world to come" which will ultimately be fulfilled in the "new heaven and

new earth" (2 Pet. 3:13; Rev.21:1).

What is man that You are mindful of him, Or the son of man that You take care of him? - This refers primarily to man and not to Christ, as a study of Psalms 8 proves. God sometimes visits man to bless him and sometimes it is to punish him.

1. Ruth 1:6 - He visited His people in the O.T. in giving them bread.
2. Lk. 1:68 - God visited and redeemed His people by sending Jesus.
3. Acts 15:14 - Peter declared that God visited the Gentiles to make out of them a people for His name.
4. James 1:27 - This verse shows that the word visit means more than just paying a call.
5.   Ps. 89:32 – "Then will I visit their transgressions with the rod." Sometimes He visits in punishment.
6. Ex. 20:5 - Visiting the iniquity of the fathers upon the children.
7. Heb. 2:6 - God visits man in order to help him and take care of him.
8. What is man that God - who is all wise, all powerful, and omnipresent - is even interested in him?

Verse 7: *You have made him a little lower than the angels* - In God's order of creation, man is of a lower order than the angels. Second Peter 2:11 says angels are greater in power and might than man.

You have crowned him with glory and honor, And set him over the works of Your hands - Adam, in his pre-sin state, was given dominion over all things that God had made.

1. Gen. 1:26-28 - He had dominion over all the earth.
2. Gen. 2:15 - He was put in the garden to keep and dress it.
3. Psalms 8:6-8 - He had dominion over the works of God's hands.

Verse 8: *You have put all things in subjection under his feet* - All things were under the dominion or rule of Adam. See again Genesis 1:26-28 and Psalms 8:4-8.

But now we do not yet see all things put under him - In the beginning, everything in the sea, air, and earth was entirely under the control of man. But now since man sinned, who would dare go into the jungle unarmed?

1. This proves that man no longer has the dominion that he once had or that God intended for him to have over His creation.
2. He lost his exalted state through sin.
3. Now we don't see all things completely under his control, but, says Paul, we do see Jesus who became man that He might die for man, redeem him from sin and ultimately restore all things as God intended in the beginning including man's dominion over God's creation (Acts 3:21).
4. This will be finally accomplished in the "new heaven and new earth." Man started in the garden of God (Gen. 1-2) and he will wind up in the garden of God when the curse of sin is removed and creation is restored (Acts 3:21; Rev. 22:1-5).

Verse 9: *But we see Jesus* - Christ came to restore man to his original dominion and power which will be ultimately fulfilled in the new heaven and new earth.

who was made a little lower than the angels - Jesus did not become an angel, but a man. He became a human being.

1. Heb. 2:16-17 - He took not on himself the nature of angels but the seed of Abraham. He became a descendant of Abraham who was a man—not an angel.
2. Phil. 2:7 - Christ was made in the likeness of man.

3. Heb. 2:14 - He became a partaker of flesh and blood.

for the suffering of death - This is exactly why Jesus became a man. He became a man so that He could suffer and die for the sins of mankind. Angels cannot die, hence, Christ became a man, so that he could die and pay the penalty that justice demanded for sin.

crowned with glory and honor, - Christ was crowned with glory and honor after His resurrection and ascension.

that He, by the grace of God, might taste death for everyone. - It was because of the grace or unmerited favor of God that Christ was sent to taste (experience) death for every man.

1. Eph. 2:8-9 - By grace are you saved.
2. Titus 3:5 - By His mercy He saved us.
3. 2 Cor. 8:9 - It was by the grace of Christ that he was willing to die.

Verse 10: *For it was fitting for Him, for whom are all things and by whom are all things* - I believe this refers to Christ.

1. Eph. 3:9 - God created all things by Jesus Christ.
2. Col. 1:16 - All things were created by Him and for Him.
3. Heb. 1:3 - By the agency of the Son, the Father made the worlds.
4. God created everything by Christ and "for Christ." He is "heir" of all things (Heb. 1:1-3). And we are joint heirs with Him (Rom. 8:16-17).

in bringing many sons to glory - Christians are sons of God and are to be brought to glory or heaven by Jesus.

1. He is the way men will get to heaven.
2. They must be bought and brought by Him.
    a. 1 John 3:1 - Christians are "sons of God."

     b. Col. 3:4 - We shall appear with Christ in glory (heaven).

     c. John 14:6 - Jesus is the way to heaven and without Him, there is no going.

to make the captain of their salvation - Christ is the captain, or author, of our salvation.

    1. Heb. 12:1-2 - He is the author and finisher of our faith.
    2. Heb. 5:9 – He is the author of eternal salvation.

perfect through sufferings. - Jesus was made perfect through His suffering.

    1. Lk. 24:46 - It was necessary for Him to suffer.
    2. Heb. 5:8 - His suffering made Him perfectly qualified to redeem us from sin and to serve as our merciful High Priest (v.17).
    3. Jesus, because He suffered, knows what it is like to:
       a. Be despised and rejected (Isa. 53:3).
       b. Be rejected by His own (John 1:11-12).
       c. Be misunderstood (John 6:60-66).
       d. Be called crazy (Mk. 3:21).
       e. Weep for others (John 11:35; Lk. 19:41).
       f. Be sorrowful and heavy hearted (Matt. 26:28).
       g. Be betrayed by a friend (Matt. 26:47-50).
       h. Suffer and die on a cross (Matt. 27).

Verse 11: *For both He who sanctifies* - This refers to Jesus. Christ sanctifies.

    1. Eph. 5:25-26 - Christ sanctifies and cleanses the church.
    2. Heb. 10:29 - Christians are sanctified by the blood of Jesus.
    3. Heb. 13:12 - Jesus sanctifies Christians with His own blood.

4. Christians are "set apart" and made holy by the sacrifice of Jesus.

and those who are being sanctified - This refers to Christians.

1. 1 Cor. 1:2 - Christians are sanctified in Christ Jesus.
2. John 17:17 - They are sanctified by the truth.
3. 1 Cor. 1:2 - They are members of the church.
4. 2 Cor. 3:17-18 - We are also being sanctified or transformed by the Spirit.

are all of one - All have the same Father and are members of the same family.

1. Matt. 6:9 - Jesus taught His disciples to pray, "Our Father."
2. John 17:21 - Jesus prayed that Christians would be one in Him and His Father.
3. Gal. 3:26, 27; 1 John 3:1 - Christians are members of the family of God. They are God's children.

for which reason He is not ashamed to call them brethren - Because we are one with Christ and we all have the same Father, Jesus is not ashamed to call us "brothers."

1. Notice that Jesus is higher than angels, while man is lower than angels and, yet, He is not ashamed to call us His brothers and sisters.
2. Matt. 12:50 - Those who do the will of the Father are His brothers and sisters and mother. That is, they are members of His family.

Verse 12: saying: "I will declare Your name to My brethren; In the midst of the assembly I will sing praise to You." Jesus declared God to us (Jn. 1:18) and He praises God with us.

1. Matt. 18:20 - Jesus is with us in a special way when we are together.

2. Matt. 26:29 - Christ drinks of the cup with us in the kingdom, just as He sings with us - in a spiritual sense because He is with us (Matt. 28:20).

Verse 13: "And again: I will put My trust in Him" - This refers to another quotation from the Old Testament and may be a quote from Psalm 18:2.

1. Matt. 27:43 - The chief priests, scribes, and elders knew that Jesus "trusted in God."
2. 1 Peter 2:21 - Christ is our perfect example of trust.
3. The children are to trust the Father as Christ did (Heb. 3:12; Eph. 1:13).

And again - This refers to another statement in the Old Testament and may refer to Isaiah 8:18.

1. The quotation, "I and the children which God hath given me," applied to Isaiah and his children when it was first spoken, but it is here applied to Christ.
2. Hosea 11:1; Matt. 2:15 - Many Old Testament prophecies had a primary and ultimate fulfillment.

Here am I and the children whom God has given Me - The Father gives the children to Christ. The children (Christians) are given to Christ by the Father because Christ purchased them.

1. John 6:37 - "All that the Father gives me...»
2. John 17:9 - Jesus prayed for them which the Father gave Him.
3. John 17:12 - God gave the apostles to Christ.

Verse 14: *Inasmuch then as the children have partaken of flesh and blood, He Himself likewise shared in the same* - He became one of us - a man in a fleshly body.

1. Heb. 10:5 - There was a human "body" prepared for

Him.
2. Phil. 2:5-7 - He was found in fashion as a man.

that through death He might destroy him who had the power of death, that is, the devil - Jesus became a man so that He might die for man's sins.

1. In dying on the cross, He delivered men from the power of sin and Satan by redeeming men from sin.
    a. Through His death, Christ destroyed the "power of death" the devil had.
    b. Jesus proved by His death that He had power over death and authority over the grave. His resurrection assures our resurrection (1 Cor. 12:22-23).
2. Christ, by His death, reduced to nothing the power that death had over man.
    a. 1 John 3:8 - Jesus was manifest that he might destroy the works of the devil.
    b. Rev. 20:10 - The devil himself will be finally destroyed.

Verse 15: *and release those who through fear of death were all their lifetime subject to bondage* - Jesus delivers us from the fear of death.

1. Men are bound by the fear of death, but Christ delivers us from the fear by providing hope.
2. Men dread death, it haunts us, but Christ showed us (by His death and resurrection) that He has power over death.
3. We are looking for Him to be with us even in death.
    a. Ps. 23:4 - Even though I walk through the valley of the shadow of death, I will fear no evil for You are with me.
    b. Phil. 1:21 - We depart and be with Christ.
    c. Bondage to sin could be included since it is the cause of the "fear of death."
    d. John 8:34 - Those who commit sin are the

servants of sin.

e. **Rom. 6:16, 17 - Christ delivers us from bondage to sin also. (See John 8:32)**

f. **Sin and bondage to it would mean that men would be lost in hell (Matt. 25:46). Christ delivers us from the wrath to come also (1 Thess. 1:10).**

Verse 16: For indeed He does not give aid to angels - Christ did not become an angel. He did not come to help angels.

1. **Heb. 2:9 – He experienced death for men, not angels.**
2. **This verse seems to me to teach that angels could not repent and be forgiven once they sinned. (2 Pet. 2:4; Jude 1:6).**

but He does give aid to the seed of Abraham - He became a descendant of Abraham or a human being in order that He might help man.

Verse 17: *Therefore, in all things He had to be made like His brethren* - This means that it was necessary for Him to become a man in order to die for sins and be a merciful High Priest.

that He might be a merciful and faithful High Priest in things pertaining to God - The High Priest had to have sympathy on others. He had to know how to sympathize with others when they were in trouble.

1. **Christ became a man and lived as a man so that He could experience what man had to experience.**
2. **Because He became a man, He knows what it is like to be tempted, hurt, neglected, rejected, etc.**
   a. **Heb. 3:1 - Jesus is our High Priest.**
   b. **Heb. 10:21 - He is High Priest over the house of God (that is, the church).**
   c. **Heb. 2:17 - He is a faithful and merciful High Priest.**

to make propitiation for the sins of the people - It was necessary for Christ to be made like His brethren so that He could make reconciliation (propitiation/satisfying justice) for sins of the people.

    1. 1 John 2:2 - Christ is the propitiation (atoning sacrifice) for our sins.
    2. Rom. 3:25 - Christ is our propitiation for sins. His death satisfies for the penalty that our sins deserve.

Verse 18: *For in that He Himself has suffered, being tempted* - Men who are honest and who really try to do what's right, when they are tempted to sin, undergo great distress of the soul. That is, they suffer anguish of mind.

    1. Heb. 4:15 - Christ was tempted as we are.
    2. Matt. 4; Lk. 4 - These chapters record His temptation in the wilderness.
    3. Matt. 16:23 - His temptation in the wilderness is by no means all the temptation He suffered. He was tempted all of His life and sometimes by His disciples.

He is able to aid those who are tempted - Because Jesus has been tempted, He is able to aid/help/relieve those that are tempted.

    1. As our High Priest He can say, "I know what it is like" and "I know what they are going through."
    2. And because He knows, He can help and aid us when we are tempted.

HEBREWS
CHAPTER THREE

JESUS IS SUPERIOR TO MOSES (Heb. 3:1-18)

Special Note: In this chapter, the writer proves that *Jesus is superior to Moses* **and then he warns them against the sin of unbelief and departing from God (Heb. 3:1-19).**

Verse 1*: Therefore* **- Seeing that Christ is so exalted as the first and second chapters show.**

holy brethren **- This shows that "Hebrews" was written to Christians. It is Christians who are "holy."**

1. **Heb. 12:14 - Christians are to follow "holiness."**
2. **1 Peter 2:9 - Christians are a "holy nation."**
3. **Eph. 1:4 - Christians should be holy.**
4. **1 Peter 1:15-16 - "Be ye holy in all manner of conduct."**
5. **2 Peter 3:11 – Christians ought to be holy.**
6. **Eph. 5:27; Col. 1:22 – Jesus keeps us holy and without blemish as we seek to be holy in our behavior.**

partakers of the heavenly calling **- The call of the gospel is a heavenly calling because it is from heaven (1 Peter 1:12), and it leads those who accept it to heaven.**

1. **Acts 2:39 - God calls men.**
2. **2 Thess. 2:14 - He calls them by the gospel.**
3. **1 Cor. 1:2 - He calls them to be saints.**

consider the Apostle **- The word "apostle" means "one sent." Christ was sent by the Father into the world to save man.**

1. **John 3:34 - "He whom God hath sent..."**

2. Gal. 4:4 - „God sent forth His Son...."
3. 1 John 4:14 - "The Father sent the Son to be the Savior of the world."
4. Matt. 15:24 - Strictly speaking He was sent to the lost sheep of the House of Israel. This is probably why he is called the "Apostle" to the Hebrews.

and High Priest of our confession, Christ Jesus - Jesus is the Christian's High Priest.

1. Heb. 10:21 - He is High Priest over the church or His house.
2. 1 Tim. 3:14-15 – The church is the house or family of God.
3. Heb. 2:17 - He is a faithful and merciful High Priest.

Verse 2*: Who was faithful to Him that appointed Him* - Jesus was faithful to do what God had appointed for Him to do.

1. John 6:38 - He came down from heaven to do the will of the Father.
2. John 9:4 - He worked the works of Him that sent Him.
3. John 17:4 - He finished the works the Father gave Him to do.
4. John 19:30 - He said, "It is finished."
5. Rev. 1:5 - Jesus is the faithful witness.

as Moses was also faithful in all his house - The Hebrews (Jews) knew that Moses was faithful to God. He was not perfect but he was faithful. In Numbers 12:7 God said, "He is faithful in all my house."

Verse 3*: For this One has been counted worthy of more glory than Moses* - These Hebrews would have known that Moses was worthy of glory and honor. In their eyes, Moses was as great as any. But the writer states that Christ is worthy of more glory than Moses. That is, *"Jesus is superior to Moses."*

inasmuch as he who built the house has more honor than the house - A man who builds a house is far superior, and much more important, than the house itself.

1. Numbers 12:7 - Moses was part of the O.T. house or family of God.
2. Matt. 16:18 - Christ built the New Testament church/house.
3. 1 Tim. 3:15 - The New Testament house is the church.
4. Noah built the ark and was counted more important than the ark (Heb. 11:7). In the same way, Jesus, who was the house builder of Israel, as well as the church, is more glorious than Moses, a member of the house of Israel, even as the builder of a house is superior to the house he builds.

Verse 4: *For every house is built by someone, but He who built all things is God* - Every house has a builder, but the builder of all things is God.

1. Acts 17:24 - God "made the world and all things there-in..."
2. Col. 1:16 - „By Him (Christ) were all things created that are in heaven and that are in earth..."
3. Heb. 1:1-12 – He had already shown that Jesus is God and Creator.

Verse 5: *and Moses indeed was faithful in all His house as a servant* - Moses served God faithfully in his O.T. house, as a servant.

1. Numbers 12:7 - He was a faithful servant in God's house.
2. Numbers 20:7-12 - He did sin. He was not perfect but he was faithful.
3. Heb. 11:24-29 – He lived by and was an example of faith.

for a testimony of those things which were to be spoken after-ward - Moses was a type of Christ. His faithfulness as a servant was a type of that of Christ. Moses was a forerunner of Christ who was to come after. Moses' life was a testimony of those things which were later to be spoken of Christ.

1. Deut. 18:15-18 – There was going to be a prophet like Moses.
2. Acts 3:22-23 - Peter said that Jesus was that prophet like Moses.

Verse 6: *But Christ as a Son over His own house* - Moses was a servant in God's O.T. house, while Christ is the Son over His N.T. house. This shows that "Christ is superior to Moses." Heb. 10:21 - Christ is High Priest over the house of God.

whose house are we - Christians are God's house or family.

1. 1 Peter 2:5 - Christians are the spiritual house of God.
2. 1 Tim. 3:15 - The house (family) of God is the church.

if we hold fast the confidence and the rejoicing of the hope firm to the end - Notice "if" we hold fast. Many of the Hebrews were about to return to Judaism as a means of justification, and Paul lets them know that they must hold fast (stay faithful) unto the end of their lives. Christians can fall from grace.

The entire book of Hebrews was written to keep them from falling (returning to Judaism and thus falling from grace). If they could not fall, why write this book?

1. Rev. 2:10 - We must be faithful until death.
2. 1 Cor. 10:12; 2 Peter 1:10 - Christians can fall.
3. Gal. 5:4 - Some of the Galatians had "fallen from grace." (See also Ezek. 33:11-19; 18:24, 26.)

Verse 7: *Therefore* - Take warning from the fate of Israel. The Israelites failed to enter the Promised Land because of unbelief. This same thing could happen to these Hebrews.

(as the Holy Spirit says) - This is a quotation from what the Holy Spirit said through David in Psalm 95:7.

1. 2 Sam. 23:2 - The Spirit spoke through David.
2. Acts 1:16 - The Holy Spirit spoke by the mouth of David.

Today, if you will hear His voice - David warned the people of his day not to harden their hearts, but to listen to God. The same warning would apply to the Hebrews. Men always want to do better tomorrow, but God says hear His voice "today." Right now is all we are ever promised as to time. Heb. 1:1-2 - These Hebrews needed to hear His voice as He spoke through His Son.

Verse 8: *do not harden your hearts as in the rebellion* – There were many times that the Israelites rebelled against God in the wilderness. These Hebrews are warned not to provoke God, by hardening their hearts and rebelling against God, as the Jews did in the wilderness.

1. Num. 13:33; 14:2; Deut. 1 - This may be what he is referring to.
2. Ex. 17 - It could be this occasion.
3. 1 Cor. 10:1-13 - It is similar to this.
4. It may refer to all of the above as well as other times.

in the day of trial in the wilderness - That is, the trying of God in the wilderness.

Verse 9: *when your fathers tested me, tried me* - When they were in the wilderness, God gave them water, manna, quail, the cloud, the pillar of fire, food, guidance, protection, etc. Yet, they kept complaining and asking, "Where is His power?"

1. This attitude and lack of faith increased their guilt and caused God to punish them as He said He would.
2. Illustration: Trial by proving. A little boy says to him-

self, "Father has forbidden me to do this, and says I will be punished if I do. But I do not believe it. I will do what he said not to do, and see if he will." The action of Israel was a trying thing on God's patience, but it proved that God meant what He said.

and saw my works forty years - This refers to the manna, quail, water from rock, brazen serpent, punishment, etc.

Verse 10*: Therefore I was angry with that generation* - That is, God was displeased with them.

and said, they always go astray in their heart - They went astray from the way He taught them.

and they have not known my ways - "Known" means more than just "knowing about" His ways. They didn't "know" them in the sense of doing them. 2 Peter 2:20-21 speaks of some who had "Known the way of righteousness..." which means experienced the righteousness of God.

Verse 11: *so I swore in my wrath, they shall not enter into my rest* - The "rest" here refers to the "rest" that the Israelites were to have in the land of Canaan. In Numbers 13:23, God said the generation who provoked Him would not have that rest.

Verse 12: *Beware, brethren* - Heed what happened to them. Profit by their mistake.

lest there be in any of you an evil heart of unbelief in departing from the living God - Many of these Hebrews were about to make the same mistake the Jews of Moses' day made. That generation did not believe and obey what God had said to them. And these Hebrew believers were about to depart from what God had said to them through His Son, Jesus.

1. Jude 1:5 - We can fall by not continuing to believe

what He says to us - just as they did.
2. Mk. 16:14 - Unbelief is the sin that hardens the heart.
3. Acts 19:9 – These were hardened by failing to believe.
4. 1 Cor. 10:1-12 - Some of the Israelites fell, and so can Christians.
5. Heb. 12:1 – Unbelief in the context of Hebrews is the "sin that so easily ensnares us."
6. We will not be lost because of weakness, ignorance, or honest misunderstanding, but we will be lost if we have an evil heart of unbelief and depart from God.

NOTE: See Appendix #2 concerning "The Security of the Believer."

Verse 13: *but exhort one another daily while it is called today* - That is, they were to encourage or give a pep talk to each other daily while they still had time - because we can be hardened against God through the deceitfulness of sin.

lest any of you be hardened through the deceitfulness of sin - Although sin may appear harmless and/or good, it is still destructive to man and his happiness.

1. Gen. 3:1-6 - Sin looked good to Eve, but it deceived her.
2. Rom. 7:11 - Sin deceived Paul.
3. Sin will take you further than you want to go and will teach you more than you want to know. It will keep you longer than you want to stay and cost you more than you want to pay.

Verse 14: *For we have become partakers of Christ, if we hold fast the beginning of our confidence steadfast to the end* - There is a sense in which we are partakers of Christ now, and we will be made partakers of Him after we endure to the end.

1. We are partakers of the benefits of His death now, and will be partakers of His glory in heaven.
2. We have eternal life now (1 John 5:11-12; 1 John

2:25), and we will have it in the world to come
(Mark 10:30).

3. We have salvation now (Mk. 16:16; 2 Tim. 1:9), and
we will be saved eternally in the end (1 Peter 1:9).

4. We are in the kingdom now (Col. 1:13; Rev. 1:9),
and we will enter the eternal state of the kingdom
(2 Peter 1:11; 3:13)

5. We are partakers of Christ now and we will be
partakers of Him in heaven.

6. "If" we hold fast. These Hebrews were on the
verge of apostasy. They were about to return to
Judaism which at that time was a glorified form of
legalism. They were encouraged by the Holy
Spirit, through Paul, to hold fast to the end.

Verse 15: *while it is said, Today if you will hear His voice do not harden your hearts, as in the rebellion* - Today is the time to do something. We need not do as they did in the wilderness. We must not harden our hearts as they did.

Verse 16: *For who, having heard rebelled* - That is, some, when they were in the wilderness, heard God, but they didn't listen. They rebelled against Him by disobeying Him and thus they provoked Him.

indeed was it not all that came out of Egypt led by Moses - Not all who came out of Egypt provoked God. Most of those numbered for war did rebel. There were exceptions, such as Joshua and Caleb and there may have been others. Deuteronomy 1:35-38 states that both Joshua and Caleb were faithful. They believed God and were allowed to enter Canaan.

SPECIAL NOTE: Not all of those who died in the wilderness were lost. Moses himself did not make it to Canaan, and there were probably some other Israelites who repented as in the case of Moses. Moses sinned in the wilderness (Numbers 20), yet, he repented; and although he didn't make it to Canaan, he still did not die lost. In this same way there were other

Israelites who sinned, repented, and although they still were not allowed to go into Canaan, they didn't die lost.

Verse 17: *Now with whom was He angry forty years? Was it not with those who sinned, whose corpses fell in the wilderness* – The writer here asked the Hebrews, "Who was God displeased with?" He answers, "It was with those who sinned (by failing to believe God)." These are the ones who died in the wilderness.

1. Numbers 14-15 - God was displeased with those who didn't believe what He said about the Promised Land.
2. 1 Cor. 10:5 - Paul says that with many of them (the Israelites) God was not well pleased.
3. Numbers 14:32 - God said they would die in the wilderness.

Verse 18: *And to whom did He swear that they would not enter into His rest, but to those who did not obey* - It was those who sinned, because of their lack of faith in God, who were not allowed to enter into the "rest" in Canaan.

1. Numbers 14:22-30 - God swore that those who dis obeyed and provoked Him (by not believing Him) would not enter Canaan.
2. Canaan was a land of rest.
   a. No more bondage or oppression, and no more wildernesses.
   b. In Canaan, there were farms, vineyards, and cities which the Israelites were to have that they did not build nor work for.
3. Heb. 3:12 - These "Hebrews" needed to see that, as those Israelites had failed to enter Canaan, be cause of their lack of faith in what God said, they would fail to enter heaven (chap. 3), if they failed to believe what God said to them.

Verse 19: *So we see that they could not enter in because of unbelief* - They did not enter Canaan because they failed to believe what God said. Here are some suggested reasons for their unbelief.

1. Fear of hunger, thirst, and other physical dangers.
2. They exaggerated the dangers that confronted them. For example, they said the men of Canaan are "giants" and we are as "grasshoppers. They said the Canaanites have cities with "walls up to heaven" (Deut. 1:28; Numbers 13:32-33).
3. They thought they could not stand against their enemies.
4. They accepted what the ten spies said, rather than what God had said. God had said "go up and take the land," but the ten rebellious spies said "we can't do it."
5. They did not trust God to the point of obeying God.
6. Heb. 3:12 - These "Hebrews" needed to take heed lest they, too, fail to believe what God has said through His Son. To fail to remain faithful would be to depart from the living God. (This is exactly what these Hebrew Christians were on the verge of doing. They were tempted to depart from God by returning to Judaism.)

HEBREWS
CHAPTER FOUR

JESUS IS SUPERIOR TO JOSHUA (Heb. 4:1-13)

Special Note: In this chapter the writer demonstrates that
"Jesus is superior to Joshua." Jesus leads Christians into a
"greater rest" than the "rest" that Joshua led the Israelites
into in Canaan (Heb. 4:1-11).

Verse 1: *Therefore, since a promise remains of entering His
rest, let us fear* - "Fear" in this verse does not mean "running
scared." It is not a fear that makes us frightened," but one
that fills us with concern and alertness.

    1. To illustrate the difference: I would be afraid to betray
       the trust my wife has in me by being unfaithful to her.
       However, I am not actually "scared" of her.
    2. Acts 10:35 - Those who fear God are accepted by Him.
    3. Rom. 11:20; Heb. 12:28 - Christians are to fear—a fear
       that causes concern and alertness.
    4. Heb. 11:7 - Noah moved with fear.

lest any of you seem to have come short of it - In chapter
3:15-19, he had shown that the Israelites could not enter
into the rest in Canaan God promised them because of their
disobedience (unbelief). In this verse, he warns the Hebrew
Christians that they need to be concerned, lest they fall
short of the heavenly rest that Christ had promised them.
Revelation 14:13 - Only those who die in the Lord "rest" from
their labors.

Verse 2: *For indeed the gospel was preached to us as well as
to them* - The word "gospel" means "good news" or "glad
tidings." The Israelites had the "good news" (gospel) of an
earthly rest (in Canaan) preached to them, just as we have

the "good news" of the heavenly rest preached to us.

But the word which they heard did not profit them not being mixed with faith in those who heard it - The gospel or good news of an earthly rest in Canaan did the Israelites no good, because those who heard it did not believe what was said to the point of obeying.

1. Deut. 1:20-32 - God had told the Israelites to go up and take the land of Canaan, but they wouldn't do as He had commanded. They believed the ten spies more than God.
2. James 1:22 – We must be doers of the word and not hearers only.

Verse 3: *For we who have believed do enter into that rest* - Christians have "rest" in Christ now and they will have rest in heaven.

1. Matt. 11:28-30 - We have rest now from:
   a. Fear (Rom. 8:15).
   b. Bondage of law (Gal. 5:1).
   c. Condemnation (Rom. 8:1).
   d. Bondage to sin (Rom. 8:2).
2. Rest should be understood like salvation. We have it now and we will have it in heaven. See Mk. 16:16; 2 Tim. 1:9; Matt. 10:22; Col. 1:13; 2 Peter 1:11; Gal. 5:22; Matt. 25:21; John 5:24; Mk. 10:29-30.
3. Rev. 14:13 - Not only do we have rest now, but we also expect rest in heaven.

As He has said: "So I swore in my wrath, they shall enter my rest" - This is the same quotation as in chapter 3:11. God has sworn that those who do not believe shall not enter into the rest He has promised them. This statement is also a negative way of assuring those who remain faithful that they will enter into the rest that God has provided for them .

although the works were finished from the foundation of the world - There was a rest planned in the mind of God from the beginning of the world.

1. Rev. 13:8; 1 Peter 1:20; Eph. 1:4; 2 Tim. 1:9 - Christ was slain in the mind of God before the foundation of the world.
2. Just as Jesus was slain in the mind of God, so the "rest" was planned in His mind from the foundation of the world.

SPECIAL NOTE: Beginning in verse 3 and going through verse 11, the writer proves that God has a "rest" promised to His people. It was not the Sabbath "rest" (the seventh day of the week rest) nor was it the "rest" in Canaan, but it is a "rest" that remains, a *heavenly rest*. Having warned them to be faithful, He now proves that there is a heavenly *rest* promised them. He does this in the following manner.

1. Verse 3 - There was a "rest" prepared in the mind of God from the foundation of the world.
2. Verses 4, 5 - It was not the seventh day rest for, after they started resting on the Sabbath day, God was still talking about men who shall enter into His rest. It was a "rest" that He would provide for them that they had not received at that time.
3. Verse 6 - There is a rest remaining, and those who had the good tidings first preached to them did not enter, because of unbelief.
4. Verses 7, 8 - After they had already begun the seventh day "rest" and the "rest" in Canaan, God through David, in Psalms 95:7-8, was still talking about another "rest" (which was the rest in heaven). If the rest that God had planned was the "rest" in Canaan, then after Israel had entered that "rest," God would not later in Psalm 95:7-8 have talked about another "rest.
5. Verses 9-11 - The "rest" that remains is the "rest" in heaven that God had planned for His people from the

foundation of the world. It is rest in the "new heaven and new earth" (2 Pet. 3:13ff; Rev. 21-22).

Verse 4: *For He has spoken in a certain place of the seventh day in this way* - The place is Genesis 2:2-3.

1. Ex. 31:17 - God rested on the seventh day.
2. Ex. 20:8-11 - Israel was commanded to keep the seventh day holy, and they were reminded that God rested on the seventh day of creation.

And God rested on the seventh day from all His works - God resting on the seventh day was a type of the rest in heaven for us. God rested from His labor (Gen. 2:3) and in heaven; we will rest from our earthly labors (Rev. 14:13).

SPECIAL NOTE: Concerning the seventh day or Sabbath, the Bible teaches:

1. Gen. 2:2-3 - God set the day apart because He had rested on that day. Note that Genesis 2:2-3 does not say *when* God sanctified the day. It was not set apart as far as man's observance was concerned until the Israelites came out of Egyptian bondage.
2. Ex. 20:8-10 - The Sabbath is the seventh day of the week and not the first day.
3. Ex. 16:22-23 - This shows that they had not been keeping the Sabbath as a "holy day" prior to this time. There is no example of Abel, Noah, Abraham, Isaac, Jacob, Joseph or any of the faithful observing the seventh day of the week as a Sabbath day before Israel left Egypt.
4. Ex. 34:27-28 - The command to keep the Sabbath was given to *Israel.*
5. Ps. 147:19-20 - The command was given *only* to Israel.
6. Ex. 31:16-17 - It was a *sign* between God and Israel.

NOTE - A wedding band is a "sign" between a man and his

wife. If a man gave a wedding ring to all the women he met, then it would not be a sign to him and his wife. If all nations had been commanded to keep the Sabbath, then the Sabbath could not have been a "sign" between God and Israel.

   7. Deut. 5:15 - The Israelites were to keep the Sabbath because God had delivered them from Egyptian bondage.
   8. Neh. 9:13-14 - The Sabbath was made known to Israel on Mount Sinai.
      a. Ex. 31:16-17 - The Sabbath was to last "forever," which means "throughout their generation" or throughout the Jewish Age. "Forever" is limited to "their generations" or the Jewish Age.
      b. Ex. 12:13-14 - The Passover was to be observed "forever."
      c. Ex. 30:8 - Incense was to be offered "forever."
      d. Eccl. 1:4 - Earth is going to abide "forever."
      e. "Forever" is sometimes limited to a certain period of time, as the above examples clearly show. The word "forever" is used to show that it will last "throughout" whatever time period is being considered but not necessarily eternal.
      f. Amos 8:5 - Israel asked, "when will the Sabbath be gone?"
      g. Amos 8:9 - God answered, "In that day (that is, in the day the Sabbath would be gone) I will cause the sun to go down at noon and darken the earth in a clear day."
      h. Matt. 27:45 - The earth was darkened at noon at the crucifixion.
      i. Col. 2:14-17 - The Sabbath Law was blotted out by Christ's death on cross.

Verses 5-6: *and again in this place: They shall not enter my rest* - Since therefore it remains that some *must* enter it, we are not there yet. After Israel had already entered the Sabbath Day rest and the Canaan land rest, God was still talking about entering into rest. Therefore, God could not have been talking about the seventh day rest or the rest in Canaan. There remains then a "rest" for God's people. Those to whom it was first preached did not enter because of disobedience. There remains a rest that the Israelites did not enter, because of unbelief. There are still some who must enter it. This must refer ultimately to the heavenly rest in heaven itself which will culminate in the "new heaven and new earth,"

Verse 7: *Again He designates a certain day, saying in David, Today, after such a long time, as it has been said: Today, if you will hear His voice, do not harden your hearts* - This is most likely from Psalm 95:7-8. David said this about 500 or 600 years after Israel had entered the rest in Canaan. Here he warned Israel not to harden their hearts against God, but to hear His voice. Implied in this warning is that there was still a rest that the Israelites could enter even after entering rest in Canaan. The faithful in Israel will be in the "rest" in heaven just like faithful Christians and believers of all ages. They will "inherit the earth" just as God promised but it will be the "new earth" and not this one (Ps. 37:9, 11, 22, 29, 34).

Verse 8: *For if Joshua* – The KJV has Jesus here, but the context clearly shows that Joshua is meant. Both Joshua and Jesus mean Savior.

1. Acts 7:45 - "Joshua" is referred to as "Jesus" in the KJV.
2. The book of Joshua is how the nation was blessed with tremendous success under the leadership of Joshua who replaced Moses as the leader in Israel.

had given them rest - Joshua led the Israelites into "rest" in Canaan. But God had a better rest in store for His people, as the rest of the verse shows.

1. Joshua 21:44 - God gave Israel rest in Canaan.
2. Joshua 22:4 - God gave them the "rest" He promised.

He gave it to those who were faithful.
3. They had rest, but it was not the final "rest" that God had planned from the beginning.

then He would not afterward have spoken of another day - If Joshua had given them the ultimate rest that God intended for His people to have, then He would not have spoken through David of another day of rest for His people.

1. Matt. 25:34 - God always had a "kingdom" prepared in His scheme of redemption for all the faithful of all ages, which will ultimately be fulfilled in the "new heaven and new earth."
2. Acts 3:21 – God had the "restoration of all things" in mind when the world first began because He knew what man would do and how He was going to fix it.

Verse 9: *There remains therefore a rest for the people of God.* - There is still a "rest" that God's people are admonished to enter. This "rest" is superior to the rest that Israel received in Canaan, because this "rest that remains" is the rest that God had in mind for His people from the beginning. Thus, Christ is superior to Joshua, because He leads His people into a greater rest than the rest into which Joshua led Israel.

1. Rev. 14:13 - We will rest from our labors.
2. "Rest" does not mean inactivity or laziness, but "rest" from pain, sorrow, persecution, affliction, temptation, etc.
3. Rev. 14:11; 20:10 - There is no rest for the wicked.
4. Rev. 21-22:5 – These chapters describe the ultimate rest God has for all the saved of all the ages.

Verse 10: *For He who has entered his rest* - The Christian, who dies having faithfully obeyed God, enters into God's rest.

he also ceased from His own works, as God did from His - Just as God rested from His works in creation, so the believers shall rest from their labors in this world. As certain as God rested, so certain will the Christian rest. The life of self-denial will end when one enters into rest with God.

1. Ex. 31:17 - God rested.
2. Rev. 14:13 - The Christian will rest.

Verse 11: *Let us therefore be diligent to enter that rest* - There is diligence involved in getting to heaven.

1. Matt. 7:13 - We must "strive to enter."
2. Rev. 14:13 - We rest from our labors.
3. Phil. 2:12 -13 - We must work out our own salvation as God works in us.
4. Our rest will come after our labor. The only time "rest" comes before "work" is in the dictionary. For us to sing, "O land of rest for thee I sigh," we must first work enough to get tired.

lest anyone fall according to the same example of disobedience - The majority of Israel fell and so can the Christian who fails to enter because of his unbelief.

1. 1 Cor. 10:1-12 - Israel fell and so can the Christian.
2. 2 Peter 1:5-10 - If we seek to do these things we shall never fall.

Note: More on "rest" - The Jews who entered Canaan had rest from their physical enemies, but they did not have the "rest" that Jesus provides from our spiritual enemies. I believe that we enter into "rest" today because we are "in Christ" (Matt. 11:28-30). We have "rest" from the guilt of sin, from being alienated from God, rest from the spiritual turmoil that sin causes, and rest from trying to be saved by law-keeping or living good enough. This "rest" that we have now is a type and taste of the rest that we will have after death and in heaven

(Rev. 14:13). We have "joy" now (1 John 1:4) but it is only a "taste" of the joy we will experience in heaven (Matt. 25:23).

Verse 12: *For the word of God is living* - God's word is alive. It is not a dead letter, but it is alive and active.

1. John 6:63 - Words are life.
2. 1 Thess. 2:13 - The message is the word of God and it works in men.
3. 1 Cor. 2:13 - The words that the men used in writing the Bible were selected by the Holy Spirit.

and powerful — The power of God's word is seen in the fact that: "Where there has been no 'word' there is no Christian." It takes the word to produce Christians.

1. Rom. 1:16 - The gospel (word) is the power God uses to save men.
2. 1 Cor. 6:9-11 - This shows the power of God's word to change the lives of sinful men.
3. Acts 2:37; 7:54 - The word cuts.
4. Ps. 19:7 - The word converts.
5. John 15:3 - The word cleans.

and sharper than any two-edged sword, - The word of God is penetrating and sharp.

1. Eph. 6:17 - The word is the sword of the Spirit.
2. Rev. 1:16 - In the vision that John saw of Christ "out of his mouth went a sharp two-edged sword."

piercing even to the division of soul and spirit, - This indicates the penetrating power of the word.

1. 1 Thess. 5:23 - Man has a body (physical life), soul (animal life) and spirit (immortal part of man created in God's image).
2. The sharpness and penetrating power of the word

is emphasized by saying "it can divide the soul and spirit." That must be pretty sharp since most of us do not really understand the difference much less be able to explain it.

and of joints and marrow, - The word is so sharp that its sharpness is emphasized by saying "it divides joints and marrow." That's somewhat like saying it divides flesh from bone.

and is a discerner of the thoughts and intents of the heart. - The word judges the thoughts and attitudes of the heart. It points out and exposes evil thoughts and intentions of hearts.

Verse 13: *And there is no creature hidden from His sight,* - No creature can escape God. He sees us all.

1. Gen. 3:8 - Adam and Eve tried to hide but couldn't.
2. Jonah 1-2 - Jonah tried to run, but couldn't get away from him.
3. Ps. 33:13-15 - The Lord looks from heaven and He sees all men.

but all things are naked and open to the eyes of Him to whom we must give account. - God sees and knows all things. He knows all about us, nothing is hidden from him.

1. Prov. 15:3 - The eyes of the Lord are in every place, beholding the evil and the good.
2. Ps. 139:1-16 – None escape His presence or perception.
3. Rom. 14:12 - Everyone must give account to God.
4. 2 Cor. 5:10 – It's either good works (those done in Christ) or bad works (those done by unbelievers), but not both.

SECTION TWO: THE SUPERIOR PRIESTHOOD OF CHRIST
(Chps. 4:14-10:39)

Special Note: Beginning here and continuing through chapter 10 the writer is going to show that *Jesus has superior a priesthood* by emphasizing:

1. Heb. 4:14 - He is the Son of God.
2. Heb. 4:15 - He is in heaven.
3. Heb. 5:6 - He is of a higher order than the Levitical Priesthood.
4. Heb. 5:8 - He is perfectly qualified to be our High Priest.
5. Heb. 5:9a - He obtained eternal salvation.
6. Heb. 5:9b - He obtained salvation for all.
7. Heb. 7:20-21 - He was made Priest with an oath.
8. Heb. 7:24 - He has an unchangeable Priesthood.
9. Heb. 7:25 - He ever lives to make intercession.
10. Heb. 7:26 - He is holy, harmless, undefiled, separate from sinners.
11. Heb. 7:26b – He is higher than the heavens.
12. Heb. 7:28 – He is perfected forever.
13. Heb. 8:6 – He has a greater covenant.
14. Heb. 9:14 - He offered a greater sacrifice.

JESUS IS SUPERIOR TO AARON AND THE LEVITICAL PRIESTHOOD

Verse 14: *Seeing then that we have a great high priest* – The writer had already identified Jesus as the Christian's High Priest.

1. Heb. 2:17 - He is identified as a faithful and merciful High Priest.
2. Heb. 3:1 - He is the "High Priest of our confession."

who passed through the heavens - When the Jews said to these Hebrew Christians: "You have no temple, no sacrifices, no city, and no high priest." The Christians could now answer with: "We have a great High Priest who is in heaven and appears in the very presence of God for us."

1. Acts 1:11 - Jesus went into heaven.
2. Heb. 8:1 - He is at the right hand of God in the heavens.
3. Heb. 9:24 - Christ has entered into heaven itself, now to appear in the presence of God for *us*.

Jesus, the Son of God - Not only is the Christian's High Priest in heaven, but more than that, He is the very Son of God.

1. Matt. 16:16 - He is the Son of the Living God.
2. Jn. 3:16 – He is the only begotten Son.

let us hold fast our confession - The Hebrew Christians had confessed their faith in Jesus as God's Son. They had embraced His religion—the religion that centers in Him and focuses on Him. However, they were now being tempted to renounce the confession they had made and go back into Judaism.

1. The writer reminds them that since we have this great High Priest, who is in heaven, the very Son of God, let us hold fast to that confession of our faith in Him.
2. Matt. 10:32-33 - If we continue to confess Him on earth, then He will confess us in heaven before the Father.

Verse 15: *For we have not a High Priest that cannot sympathize with our weaknesses* - Christ knows what it is like to live in the flesh. He can understand our weaknesses and sympathize with us in times of need.

1. Heb. 2:17 - He was made like unto His brethren that He might be a faithful and merciful high priest.
2. Although He is in heaven, He is not out of touch when we are in trouble.

but was in all points tempted as we are - Christ knows what it is like to be tempted, He was tempted just as we are and He understands.

1. 1 John 2:15-17 - Man is tempted in three main avenues: the lust of the flesh, lust of the eyes, and the pride of life.
2. Gen. 3:1-6 - It was through these three avenues that Satan tempted Eve as follows:
   a. She saw the tree was good for food - lust of the flesh.
   b. And that it was pleasant to the eyes - lust of the eyes.
   c. A tree desired to make one wise - pride of life.
3. Matt. 3; Lk. 4 - Jesus was also tempted in these three respects as follows:
   a. He was tempted to turn stone into bread - lust of the flesh.
   b. He was shown all the kingdoms of the world - lust of the eyes.
   c. He was tempted to jump off the pinnacle of the temple - the pride of life ("you'll really show your power").
4. Jesus was also tempted throughout His earthly ministry. The devil only left Him for a season (Luke 4:13). After the temptation in the wilderness, Satan used his representatives. See Matt. 16:23; Matt. 27:40, 42.

yet without sin - Although He was tempted in all points like we are, He still did not sin—not even one time.

1. 2 Cor. 5:21 - He knew no sin.
2. 1 John 3:5 - In Him is no sin.

Verse 16: *Let us therefore come boldly to the throne of grace -* The word "boldly" here speaks of confidence.

1. Because He can be touched with our weaknesses (v. 15) we need to come to the throne of grace and favor with confidence and courage.
2. 1 John 5:14-15 - We can have confidence and courage.

that we may obtain mercy, and find grace to help in time of need – Mercy is not getting what we deserve and we always need mercy because we always sin (Rom. 3:23). Grace involves getting what we do not earn. We need God's grace to supply our every need.

1. Man needs help when he is:
   a. Troubled (John 14:1-3).
   b. Tempted (1 Cor. 10:13; Heb. 2:18).
   c. Dying (Ps. 23).
   d. Lacking physical necessities (Matt. 6:25-34).
   e. Rejected by others. (Isa. 53:3).
2. Heb. 13:5-6 - When a Christian needs help physically, financially, spiritually, or mentally he needs to come to God for help.
3. Psalm 46:1 - He is our refuge and strength and a very present help in trouble.

HEBREWS
CHAPTER FIVE

JESUS IS SUPERIOR TO AARON

SPECIAL NOTE: Having mentioned that Christ is our High Priest in the latter part of chapter four the writer continues to demonstrate how *Jesus is superior to Aaron and the Levitical priesthood.* In the first ten verses of this chapter, he continues to discuss Jesus as a superior High Priest who was "called by God" as was Aaron, but was *superior to Aaron.* This discussion will be interrupted in verse 11, and then resumed again in chapter 7.

The center and glory of Judaism was the divinely appointed priesthood. What then had Christianity to offer on this point? The Judaizers could say, "In this new religion you don't even have a high priest. How are you going to get your sins pardoned, when you have no high priest to offer sacrifices for your sins? How are your priestly wants and needs going to be supplied?" In chapters 5-10 the Hebrew writer will answer these and other questions.

SPECIAL NOTE: In verses 1-4, He discusses the office of the Old Testament high priest.

Verse 1: *For every high priest taken from among men* - This shows that God's Old Testament high priests were ordinary men.

1. **Ex. 28 - This chapter reveals how the high priest was appointed.**
2. **Aaron and his sons were the priests with the eldest being the high priest.**

is appointed for men in things pertaining to God - The High Priest was appointed for men - that is, he was appointed to represent them in matters pertaining to God or spiritual matters. There was only one high priest at a time and he served as the "go-between" or mediator between God and man.

that he may offer both gifts and sacrifices for sins - Why are two things - "gifts" and "sacrifices" - mentioned?

1. Gen. 4:3-5 - "Gifts and sacrifices" may refer to the same offerings.
2. Likely there is a difference. "Gifts" may refer to bloodless offerings such as incense, meal, drink etc. "Sacrifices" refer to blood offerings.

Verse 2: *He can have compassion on those who are ignorant and going astray* - The Old Testament high priest was to have compassion on those who were ignorant and on those who erred or sinned.

since he himself is also subject to weakness - The high priest himself was subject to weakness, temptation, and sin.

1. Heb. 5:3 - He had to offer sacrifices for his own sins.
2. Heb. 9:7 - He offered first for himself and then for people.
3. Heb. 4:15 - The Christian's High Priest is without sin.

Verse 3: *Because of this he is required as for the people, so also for himself, to offer sacrifices for sins* - The high priest must offer for his own sins as well as for the sins of the people.

1. Lev. 4:3 - If the anointed priest sins, bringing guilt on the people, then let him offer to the LORD for his sin which he has sinned a young bull without blemish as a sin offering.
2. Heb. 7:27 - He offered first for his own sins and then for the sins of the people.

Verse 4: *And no man takes this honor to himself* - "This honor" refers to the honor of being high priest. No high priest could be self-appointed.

but he who is called by God, just as Aaron was - For one to be a high priest, he must be called of God as was Aaron.

1. Ex. 28 - This chapter reveals how the high priest was appointed.
2. Aaron was chosen by God to be the first high priest. He did not make himself priest.

Verse 5: *So also Christ did not glorify Himself to become High Priest* - This shows that Christ did not make Himself High Priest, but rather was "called of God" as was Aaron.

1. He did not take the honor upon Himself, but was appointed by God to the office.
2. Heb. 5:10 - He was "called of God a High Priest."

but it was He who said to Him: You are My Son, Today I have begotten You - This statement was made by God concerning the resurrection of Christ. The one who said this about His resurrection or His being brought forth from the grave also had something else to say and Paul quotes this in the next verse.

1. Ps. 2:7 - The statement quoted is found here.
2. Acts 13:33 - Here Paul applied Psalm 2:7 to the resurrection of Jesus.

Verse 6: *As He also says in another place* - This is a quotation from Ps. 110:4.

You are a priest forever according to the order of Melchizedek - God, who made the statement in Psalm 2:7, said something else about the Messiah in Psalm 110:4. This quotation reveals that the Messiah would be called of God as a High Priest, not after the order of Aaron, but after the order of Melchizedek. Paul will discuss Melchizedek in chapter seven. His point in this verse is to show that Christ is called of God to be High Priest.

Verse 7: *who in the days of His flesh* - That is, during the time Jesus lived on earth as a man.

1. John 1:14 - He was made flesh and dwelt among men.
2. Heb. 2:14 - He partook of flesh and blood.
3. Heb. 10:5 - He dwelt in a body.
4. Phil. 2:7-8 - He became a man.

when He had offered up prayers and supplications - Although Jesus prayed on many, many occasions the prayers of Matthew 26, that Jesus prayed in the shadow of the cross, are most likely referred to here.

1. Matt. 26:39 - "If it be possible, let this cup pass from me..."
2. Matt. 26:42 - He prayed the second time.
3. Matt. 26:44 - He prayed the third time.

with vehement cries and tears - This gives us some insight into the horrible suffering that Jesus endured even before He got to the cross. The suffering for sin that He did was much more than we can possibly realize.

1. Matt. 26:42 - "If it be possible, let this cup pass."
2. Luke 22:44 - He was in agony.
3. Luke 22:44 - "And being in agony, He prayed more earnestly. Then His sweat became like great drops of blood falling down to the ground."
4. Matt. 27:46 - Even on the cross, Jesus asked, "My God, my God, why have You forsaken me?"

to Him who was able to save Him from death - He prayed unto His Father. He was saved from death, but not from dying. He obtained what He prayed for when He was resurrected from the grave. He was saved from death. He was also given the strength to endure the suffering.

and was heard because of His godly fear - He was heard because of His godly and reverential fear and submission. He was heard because He prayed, "Your will be done" (Matt. 26:42). This shows His reverence for the Father.

1. 2 Cor. 12:8-9 - His prayer was heard and answered in the same way Paul's was - God helped Him to bear it.
2. Luke 22:43 - God sent an angel to strengthen Him.
3. He was saved "from death" by being resurrected.

Verse 8: *Though He was a Son* - Even though He is the Son of God, He still had to obey.

yet He learned obedience - That is, He experienced obedience. He learned what it was like to obey by obeying. He knows what it is like to be human and obey God. He then can sympathize with us as we try to obey.

1. We learn what an apple tastes like by tasting it.
2. Jesus "learned" obedience by obeying.

by the things which He suffered - "Suffered" must refer to all of the experiences of Christ while in the flesh. He obeyed the Father all of His life on earth and was obedient unto death, even the horrible death on the cross. He therefore knows what it is like to obey even to the point of dying. This is far beyond the obedience commanded of us.

1. Phil. 2:6-8 - He was obedient unto death.
2. Luke 24:46 - It was necessary for Him to suffer.
3. Heb. 2:18 - He suffered being tempted.

Verse 9: *and having been perfected* - By means of His suffering, He was made a perfect "Savior." He was thereby fully qualified in every respect to be our Redeemer.

    1. Heb. 2:10 - His suffering as a man perfectly qualified Him to be our High Priest.
    2. Heb. 2:17 - He knows what it is like to suffer and to obey. Therefore, He can be a faithful and merciful High Priest.

He became the author of eternal salvation - Jesus is the cause of our salvation. He is the means of eternal salvation. The Old Testament high priest could only make atonement for one year, but Christ is the author of eternal salvation. This helps to show that He is far superior to the high priest of the Old Testament system.

    1. Heb. 12:1-2 - He is the author and finisher of our faith.
    2. Heb. 2:10 - He is the captain or leader of our salvation.
    3. Heb. 10:1-4 - The high priest of Judaism accomplished only temporary salvation every year.

to all who obey Him - Jesus died to redeem "all." The high priest of the Old Testament only offered sacrifices for the sins of Israel. But Christ died to redeem *all*.

    1. Matt. 11:28-30 - He invites "all" to come.
    2. Heb. 2:9 - He tasted death for "every man."
    3. Matt. 7:21 - We must obey Him and do His will by believing in Him and receiving Him as Lord (Jn. 6:28).
    4. He is superior to the high priest of Judaism because He offers salvation to all.

Verse 10: *called by God as High Priest* - Christ did not appoint Himself High Priest. He was "called by God."

    1. Heb. 5:4 - No one takes this honor to himself.
    2. Heb. 5:4 - He must be "called of God" as was Aaron.
    3. Heb. 5:10 - Christ was "called of God."

according to the order of Melchizedek - That is, He was made a priest like Melchizedek. He was not made a priest after the order of Aaron and the Levitical priesthood, but like Melchizedek. We will learn more about Melchizedek in chapter 7. Right now, Paul is going to need to interrupt his discussion of Christ being a superior High Priest to discuss their dullness of hearing and lack of growth.

SPECIAL NOTE: The writer at this point interrupts his discussion of Christ's priesthood to discuss the failures of his Hebrew readers. This he will do in the remainder of chapter 5 and also in chapter 6. He will resume his discussion of "The Superiority of Christ over Aaron and the Levitical priesthood" in chapter 7:1.

1. Heb. 5:11-6:8 - Here the writer will rebuke them and warn them about their dullness of hearing and lack of growth.
2. Heb. 6:9-20 - In these verses, he will give them words of encouragement to help them remain faithful.
3. All preachers and teachers need to observe that he not only warned them, but also encouraged them.

Verse 11: *of whom we have much to say* - This "of whom" probably refers to Jesus and His Priesthood, not to Melchizedek. Melchizedek is only used as an illustration. Jesus and His Priesthood are the main subjects. He did not have "much" to say about Melchizedek, but he did have many things to say about Jesus Christ and His priesthood.

and hard to explain - That is, it would be hard to explain to *them.*

since you have become dull of hearing – This is the reason it would be hard to explain. Not only were parts of it somewhat difficult, but they were slow to learn. They had evidently grown tired of listening and learning.

1. Difficulty in understanding a certain subject can usually be caused by one of three things:
   a. The teacher's inability.
   b. The subject matter being deep and difficult.
   c. The hearers being uninterested and not eager to learn.
2. In the case of the Hebrews, it was not the speaker or the subject, but the hearers.
3. We need to consider the importance of hearing. We often emphasize the importance of preaching (1 Cor. 1:21; Mk. 16:15; Gal. 1:8, 9; 2 Tim. 4:1-2), but we seldom think about the importance of hearing.
4. The Bible has a lot to say about "hearing." The Lord puts great emphasis on hearing the word.
   a. Lk. 8:18 - Take heed how you hear.
   b. Mk. 4:24 - Take heed what you hear.
   c. Lk. 8:8 - He that has ears to hear, let him hear.
   d. Rev. 2, 3 - Hear what the Spirit says to the churches.
   e. Matt. 17:5 - Hear Him.
   f. Rom. 10:17 - Faith comes by hearing.
   g. Acts 3:22-23 - Those who refuse to hear will be "cut off."
5. The Bible also talks about different kinds of "hearers."
   a. 1 Tim. 4:1-4 - Those with itching ears who turn away their ears from the truth.
   b. James 1:22 - Those who hear only.
   c. James 1:25 - Those who are forgetful hearers.
   d. Matt. 13:15; Heb. 5:11 - Those who are dull hearers.
   e. Lk. 8:15 - Those who hear the word and keep it.
6. The preacher is not the only one involved in the sermon, so are the hearers.

Verse 12: *For though by this time you ought to be teachers* - They had already had time to learn enough to teach others. It had most likely been about thirty years or so since Pentecost and the establishment of the church. They should have grown in knowledge. They should have been able by now to teach others. This shows that after a time most of us should be able to teach others at least to some degree. This also proves that God expects us to be able to teach.

you need someone to teach you again the first principles of the oracles of God - Instead of being able to teach others, they needed teaching again, the elementary teaching of the gospel.

1. 1 Peter 4:11 - The "oracles of God" refers to the word of God.
2. An oracle is an authoritative teaching.
3. Acts 2 - The first principles can be learned in one sermon.

and you have come - This shows that they had not always been this way, but rather had become such. The same is often true today. Right after a Christian is converted he cannot get enough of the word; but later, many get to the point where they don't want to hear it, and forget what they once knew.

to need milk - They had become such as had need of milk or the elementary teaching of the gospel. They needed the basics of the Christian religion.

1. 1 Peter 2:2 - Milk is for babes in Christ or the recently converted.
2. 1 Cor. 3:2 - Paul also used "milk and meat" when writing to the Corinthians to refer to the elementary or simple truths as compared to the deeper things.

and not solid food - This refers to the deeper teaching of the word.

1. 2 Peter 3:15-16 - Some of the "meat" of the word is hard to be understood.

2. There is a lot of "meat" or deeper teaching in almost all of the books of the Bible.

Verse 13: *For everyone who partakes only of milk is unskilled in the word of righteousness, for he is a babe* - It is the newborn babes in Christ who are to desire the milk of the word that they may grow. These babes would not be skillful nor have much experience in the word of righteousness.

1. 1 Peter 2:2 - Newborn babes are to desire the pure milk of the word.
2. 2 Peter 3:16 - Some things are hard to understand but not the elementary teachings.

Verse 14: *But solid food belongs to those who are of full age* - The solid food or deeper teaching belongs to those who are mature in the faith.

that is, those who by reason of use have their senses exercised to discern both good and evil - The strong meat belongs to those who have used their senses to determine right from wrong. The deeper truth of the gospel is for those who are mature in the faith, those who, by constant use, have trained themselves to tell the difference between good and evil or right and wrong.

1. Heb. 5:14 - We need to seek to be of full age spiritully.
2. 1 Cor. 14:20; Matt. 18:1-3 - We need to be as children in some respects, such as humility and malice.
3. 1 Cor. 14:20 - In understanding and knowledge, we need to be mature.
4. The Hebrews had not grown in knowledge as they should have. Yet they were holy brethren and partakers of the heavenly calling. In chapter six, he will continue the subject he started in chapter 5:11 and encourage them to grow in faith and maturity.

HEBREWS
CHAPTER SIX

JESUS OFFERS SUPERIOR HOPE FOR CHRISTIANS

SPECIAL NOTE: In this chapter, the inspired author continues the subject he began in chapter 5:11 concerning their dullness of hearing and lack of growth. The emphasis in the latter part of this chapter is on the hope of heaven that Jesus gives which is an anchor for the soul - *a superior hope* that will always help us "go on to perfection" and learn as much as we can.

Verse 1: *Therefore leaving the discussion* - The first principles of the doctrine of Christ are not "left" in the sense that we forsake them. The Christian is to go forward, not backward, nor is he to remain in the same place. The meaning likely involves leaving the first principles and not to discuss them now. We "leave" the first principles like we do the alphabet, addition, subtraction, etc. We do not leave them in the sense of forsaking them because they are always useful to know, but not to always focus on them once they are really learned.

of the elementary principles of Christ - Some think that the "principles" refer to the things concerning Christ which were taught, typified, and predicted in the Old Testament. (See McKnight and Pink). However, it seems to me to be the "teaching of Christ" in the New Testament. The first principles are the first principles of the gospel of Christ.

1. Heb. 5:12 - The principles of Christ that he is talking about are the things that they would need to be "taught again" if they forgot them. A Christian would not necessarily need the Old Testament types, etc., before being taught the meat of the gospel.
2. Heb. 5:12 – The writer here refers to the *first* princi-

ples.
3. The A.S.V. renders this "wherefore leaving the doctrine of the *first principles* of Christ..."
4. Heb. 5:12 - The "principles" here discussed are those that had already been taught to these Hebrews at one time, because the writer says they needed to be taught to them "again.» Christians are not necessarily taught the types and shadows in the Old Testament, but they are taught the first principles of the gospel. If they were to forget them, they would need to be taught them again.
5. Heb, 5:12 - The types and shadows of the Old Testament are not considered part of the "milk" of the word by most Christians, because many of them are hard to understand.

let us go on to perfection - Let us go on toward maturity and full growth.

1. Matt. 5:48 - We are to strive to be *perfect.* We will never be sinless or perfect in our conduct, but we can be mature Christians as we strive for perfection.
2. 1 Jn. 1:8 - If we say we have (present tense) no sin we deceive ourselves.

not laying again the foundation - When building a house, we do not leave out the foundation, yet, to be always building it would be ridiculous. The foundational teachings of Christianity are the first principles of the gospel.

of repentance from dead works - That is, repentance from works that lead to spiritual death or separation. These would include "works of the law," since they were dead to them (Rom. 7:4, 6). The works would include "works of the flesh" that lead to death (Gal. 5:19-21). They would also include "works" that men do to try to save themselves (Eph. 2:8-10; Gal. 5:4).

1. Lk. 24:46-47 - Repentance is to be preached.
2. Acts 17:30 - All men are commanded to repent.
3. Matt. 21:28-29 – Here Jesus gave a Bible illustration of what repentance is. It is a change of will (mind) which brings about a change in action.
4. Repentance, simply stated, is deciding to turn to Jesus and away from a life of sin.

and of faith toward God - We must have faith in God as He is revealed in Christ.

1. Heb. 11:6 - Without faith it is impossible to please Him.
2. John 8:24 - We must believe in Christ.
3. John 14:1-2 - Jesus said, "Believe in God, believe also in me."

Verse 2: *of the doctrine of baptisms* - The New Testament mentions many baptisms. These Hebrews would have been familiar with at least some of these.

1. Matt. 28:18-20; Mk. 16:15-16 - The baptism of the Great Commission.
2. Matt. 3:5-6; Acts 18:25 - The baptism of John.
3. Matt. 3:11; Acts 1:5; 1 Cor. 12:13 - The baptism of the Holy Spirit.
4. Matt. 3:11 - The baptism of fire.
5. 1 Cor. 10:1 - The baptism into Moses.
6. Mk. 10:38-39 - The baptism of suffering.
7. 1 Cor. 15:29 - The baptism for the dead.

and of laying on of hands – This likely has reference to the laying on of the apostles' hands to confer miraculous gifts to others.

1. Acts 8:18 – It was through laying on of the *apostles' hands* the Holy Spirit was given. Here the reference is to the gifts given and not the Spirit Himself. All Chris-

tians receive the indwelling Spirit when they are baptized (Acts 2:38), but not the various gifts that were given by the laying on of the apostles hands.

2. Acts 6:6-8; Acts 19:1-6; Rom. 1:11; 2 Tim. 1:6 - These verses show that the apostles had the power to lay hands on others and confer miraculous gifts.

3. Acts 8:14-19 - It may be the case that only the apostles could confer these specific gifts to others.

4. Hands were laid on by others at times to appoint them for special missions or offices.

   a. Acts 13:3 - The disciples at Antioch laid hands on Barnabas and Paul, but it was not to confer miraculous gifts.

   b. 1 Tim. 4:14 - The miraculous gift was given to Timothy by the laying on of Paul's hands (2 Tim. 1:6). Paul's hands were evidently accompanied by that of the local elders. They were likely showing their approval and Paul was perhaps showing his respect for the office of the elders.

of the resurrection of the dead - This probably refers to the general resurrection as well as the resurrection of Christ.

1. Lk. 24:46-47 - Jesus rose from the dead.

2. 1 Cor: 15:1-4 - The resurrection of Christ is one of the facts of the gospel.

3. John 5:28-29 - Someday all in the graves are going to be resurrected.

4. 1 Cor. 15:35 - Paul discussed the resurrection of the righteous at length in this part of the Corinthian letter.

and of eternal judgment - This refers to the judgment at the last day when the "eternal verdicts" will be rendered.

1. Acts 24:15 - Paul reasoned of judgment to come.

2. Acts 17:30-32 - God has appointed a day to judge the world.

3. Heb. 9:27 - After death will come the judgment.
4. Matt. 25:30-46 - Jesus pictures how the judgment will be.
5. 2 Tim. 4:1 - Jesus will be the Judge.
6. John 12:48 - Those who reject the gospel will be judged by the words of Jesus.
7. Matt. 25:46 - Eternal verdicts will be rendered.
8. Jn. 8:24 – Christians will not come into judgment for their sins because Christ has already suffered for them. They are there to be welcomed and rewarded.

Verse 3: *And this we will do, if God permits* - This statement refers to what he said in verse one. What will we do if the Lord is willing? We will leave the first principles and go on to perfection. We will go on to those more mature lessons which will help Christians to grow.

SPECIAL NOTE: In verses 4-8 the writer emphasizes the consequences of falling away.

Verse 4: *For it is impossible for those who were once enlightened* - Those who were really converted. These were those who had been enlightened by the gospel and had been truly converted. If "once enlightened" does not refer to those who are Christians, how many times must one become "enlightened" to be a Christian?

1. Heb. 10:32 - The Hebrews had been "illuminated" or enlightened.
2. 2 Cor. 4:4 – The light of the gospel had enlightened them.
3. Col. 1:13 – Believers are conveyed out of the kingdom of darkness.

and have tasted the heavenly gift - Salvation in Christ is what he means.

1. Heb. 3:1 - The heavenly call has a heavenly gift.

2. Eph. 2:8-9 - Salvation in Christ is a "gift" of God.
3. John 6:33 - Jesus came down from heaven and He is the "gift."
4. 2 Cor. 9:15 - Therefore, salvation in Christ is an inexpressible gift.

and have become partakers of the Holy Spirit - This refers to the indwelling of the Holy Spirit that all Christians receive when they are baptized into Christ. The Spirit dwells in our hearts.

1. Acts 2:38 - Those who receive remission of sins are promised the gift of the Holy Spirit.
2. Acts 5:32 - The Holy Spirit is given to them that obey.
3. Gal. 4:6 - The Spirit is given because we are sons.
4. 1 Cor. 6:19 – The Spirit dwells or lives in the body of the saints.
5. Rom. 8:9-11 – If one does not have the indwelling Spirit he does not belong to Jesus.

Verse 5: *and have tasted the good word of God* - The word is food for the soul.

1. Ps. 119:103 - "How sweet are thy words unto my taste! Yea, sweeter than honey to my mouth."
2. Matt. 4:4 - Man lives by the word of God.
3. 1 Peter 2:2; Heb. 5:12-14 - The word is milk and meat for the soul.

and the powers of the age to come - The powers would include the power of Holy Spirit in His various manifestations as well as other blessings we receive as believers. The phrase "world to come" indicates that there will be an age after this one and that believers even now experience the same kind of "power" that we will experience then but not to the same degree.

1. Mk. 10:30 – There is a period called "now in this time" referring to the time when believers receive many bless-

ings for being believers (physical blessings, spiritual family members, etc.) and there is "the age to come" where they will receive eternal life in the new heaven and new earth.

2. Heb. 2:5 - The "world to come" is the age when "an entrance will be supplied to you abundantly into the everlasting kingdom of Christ" which is in the new heaven and new earth (2 Pet. 1:11; 3:13).

3. Rev. 21:1-22:3 – God and the Lamb will still be on the throne in the new heaven and new earth.

Verse 6: *if they shall fall away* – Some see a difference between "falling" and falling "away." They believe that the extent of the fall of the Christian under consideration here is "away." In other words, the man who falls (2 Cor. 10:12) might repent, but the man who falls "away" - it is impossible to get him to repent. This may or may not be the case.

1. If a Jewish Christian went back into Judaism and renounced Christ, then one could not get him to repent as long as he remained in that mind set, because he would have rejected the gospel. If one rejects the gospel then there is nothing else that could cause him to repent.

2. Another interpretation of this difficult verse is, "If a Christian falls away (in this case goes back into Judaism) it is impossible to get them to repent with the first principles of the gospel. They would have already heard, believed, and then rejected them. Therefore, it would be impossible for one to get this kind of person to repent with the first principles that he continues to reject."

to renew them again to repentance - The thing that is impossible is to "renew them again to repentance." These verses say that in some cases a Christian can fall so far away that he will not repent. If they would repent, then, of course, God would forgive them (2 Pet. 3:9). It is impossible to get those who "fall away" by continually renouncing the sacrifice of Jesus to repent. If these Jewish Christians (who were "enlight-ened," had tasted the heavenly gift, had partaken of the Holy Spirit, had tasted the good word of God, and the power of the age to come) were to reject Christianity and go back to Juda-ism, what further evidence could there be to convince them to repent? Since they cannot be persuaded by the gospel (which they have rejected), then they can't be forgiven, because they *won't* repent and turning to Jesus is essential.

1. The Bible clearly teaches that a Christian who falls can be forgiven when he acknowledges his need of forgive-ness.
    a. Acts 8:13-22 - Peter would not have told Simon to "repent and pray" if Simon could not have re-pented and been forgiven,
    b. Gal. 6:1 - A Christian overtaken by sin can be re stored.
    c. James 5:19-20 - A brother who errs from the truth can be converted.
    d. James 5:16; 1 John 1:9 - Christians can be forgiv-en if they will admit that they have sinned.
    e. Gal. 2:14 - Peter sinned and was forgiven.
2. While the Bible clearly teaches that a Christian who falls can be forgiven if he repents, it also teaches in He-brews 6:4-6 that a Christian can fall so far away by continually rejecting Jesus that he will never repent.

since they crucify again for themselves the Son of God - That is, they crucify in their own minds the Son of God afresh. When a person (Christian) rejects Jesus as the sin offering it appears that he agrees that Christ deserved to be cruci-fied as an imposter. These Jewish Christians, if they returned to Judaism, would have been saying, "Christ deserved to be crucified as a false teacher." They would crucify Him again in their minds and by their actions.

1. Heb. 10:25-31 - Willful sinning on the part of a Christian is a dangerous thing which in this context

is forsaking Jesus.
2. 2 Peter 2:20-22 – A Christian going back into sin is like a dog going back and eating his own vomit.

and put Him to an open shame - The Christian who goes back into the world or back into Judaism brings shame on Christ. He makes Christ appear powerless. He makes it appear that Christ doesn't have the power to keep those who are His. He shames Christ by renouncing Him.

1. Heb. 12:1-2 – When Jesus was crucified He endured the cross despising the shame.
2. Heb. 10:29 – Those who continue to forsake Christ count His blood a common or ordinary thing, thus putting Him to open shame.
3. It also brings shame on the church. When a ball player drops the ball, he usually feels bad, because he hurts the team.

Verse 7: *For the earth, which drinks in the rain that often comes upon it* - The earth is used here to illustrate the Christian. Just as the earth drinks in the rain, so the Christian drinks in the blessings of God.

and bears herbs useful for those by whom it is cultivated, receives blessing from God; - Herbs are symbolic of the fruit desired in the life of a Christian. Good seed and good soil with refreshment (rain) from God should produce good fruit. Likewise, Christians with refreshment (blessings) from God should bring forth good fruits. Those Christians who do bring forth good fruit will receive blessings from God.

Verse 8: *but if it bears thorns and briers, it is rejected and near to being cursed,* - Just as land that brings forth thorns and briars is rejected, so is the Christian who does not bear fruit or live faithfully.

1. John 15:1-5 - Jesus requires that His disciples bear

fruit for Him.

2. Gal. 5:22-23 – This is the fruit that the Spirit produces in us.

whose end is to be burned - Christians who do not bear fruit for God will be burned in hell.

1. John 15:6 - Fruitless branches will be gathered and burned.
2. Gal. 5:22 – The fruit of the Spirit is listed here which illustrates faithfulness.
3. Rom. 6:22 – Fruit is holiness which can only come from faithfulness.

SPECIAL NOTE: Beginning in verse nine the writer declares his hope for them. He first rebukes them and points out those things wrong with them (5:11-6:8), then he encourages them by expressing his confidence in them, and by assuring them of salvation in Christ (vs. 9-20).

1. Heb. 13:25 – When he finishes this book he will express "grace to all."
2. 2 Thess. 2:1-13 - Paul's manner of softening hard statements is seen by some as further evidence that he wrote the book of "Hebrews."

Verse 9: *But, beloved, we are confident of better things concerning you,* - That is, he was confident that better things would come forth from these Hebrew Christians other than apostasy and bringing forth bad fruit.

yes, things that accompany salvation, though we speak in this manner.- They had been saved from their past sins and should continue to do the things that God desires of Christians.

1. Mk. 16:16 - Those who believe and are baptized are saved from their sins.
2. 2 Peter 1:5-11 - As Christians we are to seek to add the

Christian graces that go along with our salvation.

   3. Eph. 2:10 – Things that accompany salvation are the good works that God has appointed for us to do.

Verse 10: *For God is not unjust to forget your work and labor of love* - Paul here reminds them that God will not forget their work and labor. Although these Hebrews had neglected studying and had not grown in knowledge as they should, they had done some good things for Christ and His cause.

   1. Gen. 40:23 - Men often forget our good deeds, but God won't.
   2. Eph. 2:10; 1 Cor. 15:58a - Christians are to abound in work of the Lord.
   3. 1 Cor. 15:58b - We are assured that if we remain faithful our labor will not be in vain. God will not forget.
   4. Rev. 14:13; 1 Cor. 3:8 - Our works follow us in death and we will be rewarded for them.

which you have shown toward His name, - They had shown their love for Christ by showing love for others.

in that ye have ministered to the saints, and do minister - They had, in times past, ministered to the saints, and they still did when the writer wrote the book.

   1. Matt. 25:40 - We are to help one another.
   2. 1 John 3:17 - The love of God does not dwell in those who refuse to help other believers.
   3. 1 Cor. 16:1-2 - We are to help saints when they are in need, but there is no passage that says the church can help saints only.
   4. Gal. 6:10 - This verse teaches that Christians (individually or collectively) are to help not only saints, but also "all men.»
   5. 2 Cor. 9:12-13 - These verses teach us that we can help saints and all men.

Verse 11: *And we desire that each one of you show the same diligence* - He desired that every one of them continued the same diligence. Christianity is an individual religion.

1. Acts 2:38 - Everyone must be baptized.
2. Rom. 14:12 - Everyone shall give account to God.
3. 2 Cor. 5:10 - Everyone will receive what is due for the things done in his body.

to the full assurance of hope until the end - That is, the end of life on earth or end of the world, whichever comes first. Christians must work till the end of life on earth.

1. Rev. 2:10 - We must be faithful until death.
2. Rev. 14:13 - After dying in the Lord, we rest from our labors.

Verse 12: *that you do not become sluggish,* - They were not to be sluggish or lazy.

1. Matt. 25:26-30 - The lazy servant will be cast into outer darkness.
2. There are obviously degrees of dedication and faithfulness but not to do anything is unacceptable.

but imitate those who through faith and patience inherit the promises. - The Hebrews and all Christians are to follow the example of those in times past, who through their faith in God and patient endurance received the things that God had promised them.

1. Heb. 11:1-40 - This chapter gives some great examples.
2. Heb. 10:36 - Christians need patience/endurance because after they have done the will of God, they will receive what God has promised them.

Verse 13: *For when God made a promise to Abraham* - This is the promise of Genesis 12:1-3 and repeated in Genesis 22:15-18.

because He could swear by no one greater, He swore by Himself - This refers to Genesis 22:16 where God swore by Himself.

Verse 14: *saying, "Surely blessing I will bless you, and multiplying I will multiply you."* - God made this promise to Abraham as recorded in Gen. 22:15-18.

1. God would bless him.
2. He would have numerous descendants. All nations would be blessed through his seed.
3. Gal. 3:16 – The seed or descendant who would be Christ would descend from Isaac.

Verse 15: *And so, after he had patiently endured, he obtained the promise.* - He obtained the promise so far as it pertained to his personal enjoyment. He received the promise, mentioned in verse 14 of this chapter, before he died. He received Isaac and through him the promise was obtained.

1. Abraham lived long enough to see the promise, about being blessed and having many descendants, fulfilled.
2. After waiting patiently Abraham received the promise.
3. Of course there is a sense in which he did not receive all the promise in his lifetime but he will receive it in the new heavens and new earth when Jesus returns (Rom. 4:13; 2 Pet. 3:8-13).

Verse 16: *For men indeed swear by the greater* - When men swear, they swear by someone or something greater than themselves.

and an oath for confirmation is to them an end of all dispute - That is, an oath confirms what has been said, and the oath puts an end to all arguments. When an honest man says something, and swears that it is the truth, that's it.

Verse 17: *Thus God, determining to show more abundantly to the heirs of promise* – Christians as well as believers of all previous ages are "heirs of the promise" that God made to Abraham. God wanted to really show the "heirs of the promise" the unchangeableness of that promise.

1. Gal. 3:29 - Christians are "heirs of the promise."
2. Gen. 22:18; Gal: 3:16 - The promise, in mind here, is that all nations would be blessed through the "seed" of Abraham and that "seed" is Christ.
3. Rom. 4:13; Heb. 9:15 – Abraham and all of his descendants (those who had/have the faith of Abraham) are heirs of the promise God made about Jesus.

the immutability of His counsel - God wanted to show as clearly as possible the unchangeableness of His counsel and His determination to bless all nations through Christ).

confirmed it by an oath - In order to show that He was not going to change His mind about the promise, God confirmed the promise with an oath. God, out of condescension to that human weakness which puts more confidence in an oath than in the bare word, confirmed His promise by an oath. God wanted to give the heirs of the promise all the assurance He possibly could, so He confirmed His promise with an oath. God promised that Abraham's seed (Christ, Gal. 3:16) would bless men and He assured us, in the strongest manner possible, that He would fulfill that promise.

Verse 18: *that by two immutable things* - The two unchangeable things are listed in verse 17. They are His promise and His oath.

in which it was impossible for God to lie - God cannot lie, either in His promise or His oath. Therefore, the promise is double-sure. God knew that when men swore to something, that ended all argument. So He swore that He would fulfill His promise to bless men through Christ and He cannot lie.

1.   Titus 1:2 - God cannot lie.
2.   Num. 23:19 – God is not man that He should lie.

we might have strong consolation - That is, because of God's promise and oath, those of us who are "in Christ" have strong encouragement. This would be very strong encouragement to the Hebrew Christians. This would serve to reassure them, in the strongest possible way, that they had the salvation that God had promised those "in Christ."

who have fled for refuge - Christians are the ones who have fled for refuge in Christ. Only those who have fled for refuge in Christ have this great encouragement. Those who have fled for refuge in Christ have strong encouragement, because God promised and God swore to bless those "in Christ."

1. Gal. 3:26-29 - Men are baptized "into Christ" and are thus heirs of the promise God made to Abraham.
2. Heb. 10: 23-24 - Surely this would encourage the Hebrews to remain "in Christ" and not return to Judaism.
3. Joshua 20:2-6; Deut. 19:5-6; Numbers 36:6, 11, 14 - The idea for "refuge" came from the cities of refuge. The cities of refuge in Canaan were a type of our refuge in Christ.

to lay hold of the hope set before us - The hope of the Christian is eternal life in Christ, and all Christians have this hope. We desire and expect to live eternally with God.

1. 1 John 5:11-12 - Eternal life is in the Son and those who have the Son have eternal life.

2. 1 Tim. 6:12, 19 - Christians are to lay hold on eternal life.

Verse 19: *This hope we have as an anchor of the soul* - As the anchor holds the ship when storms are raging, so this hope holds the soul steadfast.

both sure and steadfast - This anchor will hold because it is sure and it is steadfast.

and which enters the Presence behind the veil, - The veil or curtain was before the Holy of Holies in the Tabernacle, and the Holy of Holies in the Tabernacle was a type of heaven. The hope within the veil for the Christian is heaven.

1. It is a *heavenly* hope.
2. John 14:1-3 - Heaven is a place prepared for the people of God.

Verse 20: *where the forerunner has entered for us, even Jesus,-* Christians have the desire and expectation of entering into the place where Jesus went before us. The word "forerunner" means that where Christ has gone, His disciples shall at last follow.

1. 1 Thess. 1:1 - Jesus is our hope of heaven.
2. "Hope" is desire with expectation of receiving what is desired.
    a. Desire only is not hope. I might desire to win $10,000,000, but I don't expect to get it so I have no "hope" of obtaining it.
    b. Expectation only is not hope. I might expect sickness to come to my family, but I don't desire it so I don't "hope" for it.
    c. But when we both desire and expect something, then, we hope for it. The Christian both desires and expects to live in heaven eternally.

having become High Priest forever according to the order of Melchizedek. - This takes the writer back to chapter 5:10 and his discussion of the "superiority of the priesthood of Christ." Having made this statement, he will now in chapter 7 resume his discussion of the priesthood.

HEBREWS
Chapter Seven

JESUS IS SUPERIOR TO THE LEVITICAL
PREISTHOOD

SPECIAL NOTE: Beginning in chapter 7:1 and continuing through chapter 8:5, the writer resumes his discussion of the *Priesthood of Christ being superior to the Levitical priesthood.* He interrupted this discussion in chapter 5:11 to discuss the Hebrews' dullness of hearing and lack of growth. He now resumes his discussion of the superior Priesthood of Christ. The Hebrew Christians would be encouraged to continued faithfulness by the fact that the Priesthood of Christ is far superior to that of Aaron and the Levitical system. To return to the Levitical system would be to return to one that was: (1) inferior (7:1-7); (2) unable to bring perfection (7:11); (3) replaced by another of a different order (7:12-21); and (4) whose priests were sinners themselves (7:27-28).

Verse 1: *For this Melchizedek* - There have been many varying opinions of just who this man really was. Some have thought that he was pre-incarnate Christ, the Holy Spirit, an angel, Shem, Enoch, and even others. I believe that he was a man named Melchizedek, but exactly who he was is a mystery to me. This could have been an OT appearance of the Son of God. He made other appearances in Genesis (Gen. 18), but this is by no means certain.

1. Heb. 7:4 - Melchizedek was a great man.
2. Heb. 5:6, 10; 6:20; 7:1, 10, 11, 15, 17 - He is mentioned eight times in Hebrews.
3. Gen. 14:18; Ps. 110:4 - He is mentioned twice in the Old Testament.

king of Salem - Salem refers to Jerusalem. He seems to have been the actual King of Salem, since the King of Sodom is also mentioned in the same context.

1. Gen. 14:17-18 – The king of Sodom and king of Salem are both named here.
2. Ps. 76:2 - Jerusalem here is referred to as Salem. Note: Jerusalem.

priest of the Most High God - This is very important because it shows that Melchizedek was both King and Priest at the same time. Christ is a Priest after the order of Melchizedek (Heb. 6:20). Therefore, Christ is both King and Priest at the same time. According to Hebrews 3:1 and 8:1, Christ is Priest now. He is also King now and will not have to wait until His second coming to be King and Priest.

1. Zech. 6:12, 13 – Zechariah foretold this very thing when he wrote: "Behold, the Man whose name *is* the BRANCH! From His place He shall branch out, And He shall build the temple of the Lord; Yes, He shall build the temple of the Lord. He shall bear the glory, And shall sit and rule on His throne; So He shall be a priest on His throne, And the counsel of peace shall be between them both."
2. Notice that Zechariah's prophecy includes the following: There would be a man whose name is the BRANCH.
3. Jeremiah 23:5-6 identifies the Lord as the BRANCH. (See also Isaiah 11:1; Rom. 15:12; Rev. 5:5; Rev. 22:16; Isaiah 53:2.)
4. The BRANCH would build the temple of the Lord. Christ built the church (Matt. 16:18), which is the true temple of God (1 Cor. 3:16; Eph. 2:21-22).
5. The BRANCH would sit and rule on His throne. Jesus ascended into heaven and in heaven He sits (Acts 2:34) and rules (Heb. 1:8) on His throne (Heb. 1:8).
6. The BRANCH would be Priest on His throne. He would be like Melchizedek—Priest and King on His

throne. He would sit, rule, and be priest on His throne at the same time. He is Priest now (Heb. 3 :1; 4:14; 8:1); He sits now (Acts 2:34; Heb. 8:1; 12:2); therefore, He is King now (Heb. 1:8) - just like Melchizedek was.

who met Abraham returning from the slaughter of the kings - Lot had been taken prisoner by several kings, and Abraham, in rescuing Lot, had slaughtered them.

1. Gen. 14:1-20 - This is the account.
2. Observe that the writer said that Abraham slaughtered the kings. He could have said defeated, but God calls things as they are.

and blessed him - Melchizedek met Abraham when he re-turned from the slaughter of the kings and Melchizedek blessed Abraham.

1. Gen. 14:19-20 – "And he blessed him and said: "Bless-ed be Abram of God Most High, Possessor of heaven and earth; And blessed be God Most High, who has delivered your enemies into your hand.""
2. Heb. 7:7 - The lesser (Abraham) was blessed by the greater (Melchizedek).

Verse 2: *to whom also Abraham gave a tenth part of all* - From the statement in Genesis 14:20, it is hard to tell who paid tithes to whom. However, the Hebrew writer makes it per-fectly clear that Abraham gave a tenth part to Melchizedek. Observe that this giving of the tenth to the priest of God oc-curred long before the Law of Moses was given. Also, in Ge-nesis 28:22, Jacob vowed to give God the tenth, and this, too, was before the Law of Moses was given. It seems from these examples that God has never expected less than a tenth from those who would give to him. How Christians can study the Bible and then determine that they do not need to give at least a tenth is beyond me.

first being translated "king of righteousness," - Melchizedek means King of Righteousness.

and then also king of Salem, meaning "king of peace," - King of Salem means King of peace. Christ, who is a King and Priest as Melchizedek was, is our King of Righteousness and our King of peace.

1. Heb. 1:8 - He has a scepter of righteousness.
2. Isaiah 9:6, 7 - He is our "Prince of Peace." See also Luke 2:14; Acts 10:36; Rom. 5:1; John 16:33; 14:17; & Col. 1:20.
3. Rom. 14:17 - His kingdom is a kingdom of peace.
4. Matt. 5:9 - His disciples are peacemakers.

Verse 3: *without father, without mother -* Melchizedek was without father or mother as far as the inspired record is concerned. There is no *record* of his father or his mother. He did not, therefore, as did the Levitical priests, derive his priesthood from his parents, but was made priest of God by a special appointment.

without genealogy- As far as his genealogy, the Scriptures are silent. As far as the Scriptures show, he had no ancestors. This simply means that he had none as far as the record shows, not necessarily that he was born any different from other men. The Levites received their priestly offices through carefully guarded genealogies, but that was not so with Melchizedek. He was made priest by a special appointment.

having neither beginning of days, nor end of life - There is no record of his birth or his death - unlike the Levitical system which kept very strict records of both birth and death of the priests. He comes on the scene as a priest and king, and he leaves that way. As far as the record shows, he is still a priest, though not literally so.

but, made like unto the Son of God, remains a priest continually - Melchizedek, like the Son of God, abides as a priest forever. That is, like Jesus, he fills up the entire time of his priesthood himself. No one succeeded Melchizedek as priest, because he was priest throughout his entire priesthood. The word "continually" means that he continued as priest for the full period of his priesthood without interruption. Melchizedek was therefore a priest throughout his history, and there is no record of its beginning or ending. His priesthood did not cease as far as the time in which he served as a priest is concerned. None succeeded him or preceded him. He was the only one to serve as his type of priest.

1. If it were literally true that he continues as a priest even today, then we would have two kings and two priests reigning today and that is contrary to the Scriptures. For example, 1 Timothy 2:5 says there is only one mediator between God and man and that is, Jesus Christ.
2. The word "forever" is sometimes applied to a specific time and is used to include all of that time. No one succeeded Melchizedek as priest - he was priest and king all the time that he appears in Scripture or forever.
   a. Ecc. 1:4 - The earth abides "forever," yet, it will end according to Matthew 24:5 and 2 Peter 3:10.
   b. Ex. 31:16, 17 - The Sabbath was perpetual or continuing forever, but it has ended according to Colossians 2:14-16. The word "forever" in Exodus 31:16-17 is limited to "throughout the Jewish Age" and it was used to include all of the time during the Jewish Age. In like manner, Melchizedek was a priest "forever" or "throughout the entire period of his priesthood."

Verse 4: *Now consider how great this man was, to whom even the patriarch Abraham gave a tenth of the spoils* - The aim of the author is to show that the priesthood of Melchizedek is superior to that of the Levitical system. And there was no man, in the mind of the Jew, who was greater than Abraham.

However, Abraham did two things that showed him to be inferior to Melchizedek: He paid tithes to Melchizedek and he received a blessing from Melchizedek (v. 6).

1. Abraham paid the tenth of the spoils to Melchizedek, and he was the father of the whole Jewish Nation.
2. A patriarch was a father or ruler of a family or race.

Verse 5: *And indeed those who are of the sons of Levi, who receive the priesthood, have a commandment to receive tithes from the people according to the law, that is, from their brethren, though they have come from the loins of Abraham;-* The Israelites were required to pay tithes to the Levites and the Levites (the descendants of Levi) in turn paid tithes to the priests—to those descendants of Levi who were of the house of Aaron and served as priests. The Levites had a command in the Law of Moses to take tithes from the rest of the Israelites, even though they, too, descended from Abraham.

1. Numbers 18:21-36 - This is the command referred to in the law.
2. All of the priests were Levites but not all of the Levites were priests.

Verse 6: *but he whose genealogy is not derived from them received tithes from Abraham and blessed him who had the promises.-* Melchizedek had no recorded genealogy, and he did not descend from the Levites - as the Levitical priests had to do - and yet, he received tithes from Abraham, the father of the Jewish Nation. He also blessed Abraham, which shows that he was superior to Abraham and the whole Jewish Nation. Abraham had the promises yet, he was blessed by, and paid tithes to, Melchizedek. Therefore, Abraham was inferior to him.

Verse 7: *Now beyond all contradiction, the less is blessed of the better* - The meaning of this verse is "without doubt, without dispute, the less (in this case Abraham) was blessed by the better (Melchizedek)." By paying tithes to Melchizedek and receiving a blessing from him, Abraham demonstrated that he was inferior to Melchizedek and these Hebrews could not argue the point, because all know that the less is always blessed by the greater and never is it the other way around.

Verse 8: *Here mortal men receive tithes, but there he receives them, of whom it is witnessed that he lives.* - The word "here" refers to the Levitical system. The tithes paid were paid to men who died. The words "but there" seem to refer to the priesthood of Melchizedek. Some think it refers to Jesus. But the meaning of the verse seems to be: Under the Levitical system men that die receive tithes; but under the priesthood of Melchizedek, he received them and there is no record of him dying. He lives as far as the record shows. He had no end of days so far as the record is concerned.

1. The statement "he lives" may mean that he lives in type. It cannot mean that he lives and serves as priest now, in a literal sense, because that would contradict 1 Timothy 2:5.
2. He had no beginning or end as a priest, not necessarily as a person. His life may have ended as a person, but he had no end or beginning as a priest.

Verses 9-10: *Even Levi, who receives tithes, paid tithes through Abraham, so to speak, for he was still in the loins of his father when Melchizedek met him.* - The meaning of these verses seems to be as follows: Levi, whose descendants received tithes from the Israelites, paid tithes to Melchizedek through Abraham. For Levi was still in the body (so to speak) of Abraham when Melchizedek met him. In a certain sense, all the descendants of Abraham paid tithes to Melchizedek - in a representative and indirect way - when Abraham did. The main purpose of the writer is to show that the priesthood of Melchizedek was superior to the Levitical priesthood. Abraham paying tithes and receiving a blessing showed himself and all of his descendants (including the Levites) to be inferior to Melchizedek. The point of all this is simply this: The priesthood of Melchizedek is superior to that of the Levitical system. Jesus is a Priest after the order of Melchizedek. So the Priesthood of Jesus is superior to the Levitical Priesthood. Therefore, for these Hebrew Christians to return to Judaism would be to return to a priesthood far inferior to what they had as Christians.

1. Heb. 4:14a - Christians have a great High Priest who has passed into the heavens.
2. Heb. 4:14b – He is Jesus Christ the Son of God.

SPECIAL NOTE: Beginning in verse 11, the writer begins explaining the imperfections of the Levitical system. Having shown in verses 1-10 that the priesthood of *Jesus is superior to the Levitical priesthood*, he now explains *why* a change in the priesthood was needed.

Verse 11: *Therefore, if perfection were through the Levitical priesthood (for under it the people received the law),* - The priesthood and the Law of Moses were connected. They stood or fell together. It was under the Levitical priesthood that the Israelites received the law. However, God's full saving purpose was not in the Levitical priesthood and the law of Moses. The law and the Levitical priesthood could not bring man to the highest goal in religion. It could not make man as he needed to be, which is absolutely forgiven of sins and totally righteous before God.

1. Gal. 3:21 - The law (which included the Levitical priesthood) could not make men righteous nor give them life.
2. Heb. 10:4 - The sacrifices under the Levitical system could not take away sins. There was no absolute forgiveness under the law and the Levitical priesthood.

what further need was there that another priest should rise according to the order of Melchizedek, and not be called according to the order of Aaron? - His question simply stated is this: If the Levitical system brought absolute forgiveness of sins, why did God, through David in Psalms 110:4, speak of another priest arising after the order of Melchizedek and not after the order of Aaron? The very fact that God foretold through David that one day a priest was going to rise after the order of Melchizedek shows that, even during the times of the Old Testament, He intended to change from the Levitical priesthood, because, under it, there was no absolute forgiveness. If there was, then why did God say He was going to change it? The blood of Jesus would not have been needed if the Levitical priesthood, with its sacrifices and offerings, had brought forgiveness of sins.

1. Psalms 110:4 - "The Lord has sworn, and will not relent, You are a priest forever according to the order of Melchizedek." David's statement in the Old Testament showed clearly that one day God was going to change the priesthood, and the reason He changed it was because there was no absolute forgiveness under the Levitical priesthood.
2. Heb. 10:4 – It is not possible for the blood of animals to take away sin.

Verse 12: *For the priesthood being changed of necessity there is also a change also of the law* - The priesthood and the Law of Moses stood or fell together. For the priesthood to be changed, it was absolutely necessary to change the law. Why? Because the law said that the priests had to be of the tribe of Levi and the family of Aaron. Therefore, it would be impossible to change the priesthood without also changing the law.

1. Exodus 28:1 - Now take Aaron your brother, and his sons with him, from among the children of Israel, that he may minister to Me as priest, Aaron *and* Aaron's sons: Nadab, Abihu, Eleazar, and Ithamar.
2. Heb. 10:9 - Christ took away the Old Law that He might establish His New Law.

Verse 13: *For He of whom these things are spoken belongs to another tribe, from which no man has officiated at the altar.* - This verse explains why the law had to be changed. The one David was talking about belonged to another tribe and no one from that tribe was ever allowed by the Law of Moses to offer sacrifices at the altar. To offer sacrifices or serve as a priest under the law of Moses, one had to be of the tribe of Levi.

1. Heb. 7:5 - The sons of Levi are the ones who receive the office of the priesthood.
2. Matt. 1:1-18; Lk. 3:23-38 – Levi is not mentioned in the genealogy of Jesus.

Verse 14: *For it is evident that our Lord arose from Judah; of which tribe Moses spoke nothing concerning priesthood* - Jesus, the one of whom those things were spoken in Psalms 110:4, came from the tribe of Judah. Moses' law did not say anything about a man from that tribe serving as a priest. Therefore, the law had to be changed (7:12) before Christ could be a priest after the order of Melchizedek.

1. Ex. 1:1-3 - Jacob had twelve sons. The descendants of each son constituted the twelve tribes of Israel. One of Jacob's sons was named Levi. Only Levi's descendants could serve as priests. Another son was named Judah. Christ was born of his descendants.
2. Matt. 1:3ff - Joseph, the husband of Mary, was of the tribe of Judah.
3. Luke 3:23-33 - Mary also was a descendant of Judah, therefore, so was Jesus according to the flesh.

Verse 15: *And it is yet far more evident if in the likeness of Melchizedek, there arises another priest* - The meaning is: It is far more evident that God was going to change the law and the priesthood from the fact that another priest was to arise after the order of Melchizedek, and this priest was from the tribe of Judah.

Verse 16: *who has come, not according to the law of a fleshly commandment*. The Levites were made priests by their fleshly descent from Levi. Christ, however, was not made priest due to His fleshly descent. The priesthood is called a "fleshly commandment" because it was a system of earth-bound rules.

but according to the power of an endless life - Christ was made Priest, not because of His fleshly descent, but because of His endless life. David had said that He would be Priest "forever", and Jesus would fulfill that prophecy because of His "endless life."

Verse 17: *For he testifies "You are a priest forever according to the order of Melchizedek* - This is quoted from Psalms 110:4 to prove that even in the Old Testament, God had predicted this change in the priesthood, and also that Christ would be priest forever.

SPECIAL NOTE: Bear in mind that the Judaizers could say, "Look, we have the temple and the Levitical Priesthood to offer sacrifices for our sins, and what do you Christians have? Nothing!" After the reading of the Book of Hebrews, the Christians could say: "We have a High Priest who is as far superior to the Levitical priests as Melchizedek was superior to Abraham." Hence, the Hebrew Christians would have been encouraged to remain faithful to Christ and not return to Judaism. There was *better news for the Hebrews*.

Verse 18: *For on the one hand there is an annulling of the former commandment* - The former commandment refers to the Law of Moses. The old law has been set aside, abolished, and put away.

1. Eph. 2:15 - Christ abolished by His death the enmity or the law of commandments contained in ordinances.

2. Col. 2:14-16 – The curse of the old law had to be taken away.

because of its weakness and unprofitableness, - The weakness of the law was in the fact that man could not keep it perfectly, and it was unprofitable because the sacrifices offered under the law could not take away sins.

1. Gal. 3:21 - The law could not give life, nor could it make men righteous, because men could not keep it perfectly.
2. Heb. 10:4 - The sacrifices offered under the law could not take away sin.
3. Heb. 7:19 - The law made nothing perfect which means that it provided no absolute forgiveness because man could not keep it.
4. Gal. 3:10 – For one to be justified by law he must keep it in every detail at all times.

SPECIAL STUDY - While it is true that the law was weak and unprofitable, because man could not keep it perfectly, and because its sacrifices could not take away sins, it still did exactly what God intended for the law to do. God did not intend for the Law of Moses to last forever, but only long enough to accomplish its intended purpose. Like a temporary bridge - which only lasts until a better bridge is built - the law was only to last until the coming of Christ and the establishment of a better covenant. Again, the Law of Moses did exactly what God intended for it to do. The following will show this to be true:

1. The law was "holy, just, and good. (Rom. 7:12). The weakness of the law was in man's inability to keep it and the inability of its sacrifices to take away sins.
2. The law defined sin and therefore it told men what sin was (Rom. 7:7).
3. The law furnished types and shadows of what was to come (Heb. 10:1).
4. The law kept the Jews a separate race until Christ

could be born (Eph. 2:11-16).

5. The law served as a schoolmaster to bring men to
    Christ (Gal. 3:24).

6. The law therefore accomplished what God
    intended for it to accomplish, but God never intend-
    ed for the Law of Moses to provide absolute forgive
    ness of sins. Hence, it was weak and unprofitable as
    far as absolute forgiveness was concerned.

Verse 19: *for the law made nothing perfect* - There was no
perfection because of the inability of man to keep the law and
the inability of animal sacrifices to take away sin. There was
no absolute forgiveness of sin under the law.

1. Heb. 10:4 - The blood of animals did not take away sin,
    but rather "rolled sins forward" so to speak year after
    year until the blood of Christ was shed.

2. The Old Testament saints were forgiven, but the sins
    were not actually taken away until Christ shed His
    blood on Calvary.

3. Rom. 3:25-26 - Looking forward to the blood of Christ
    is the only way God could be just and yet forgive sins
    in the Old Testament.

4. Heb. 9:15 - Christ died "for the redemption of the
    transgressions that were under the first testament."
    That is, Christ died to redeem those faithful saints who
    had transgressed the law of Moses.

5. Illustration of forgiveness in the Old Testament: A man
    gives me a check on Saturday for a tire, and has set
    up direct deposit so his money will be in the bank as
    soon as the bank opens. I have my money for the tire
    because I have the check, but not in an absolute sense.
    I have it only because the money will be in the bank on
    Monday. Old Testament saints were forgiven because
    the direct deposit of the blood of Jesus had already
    been set up by God.

on the other hand, there is the bringing in of a better hope,
through which we draw near to God. - The better hope refers
to Christ and the New Covenant. The better hope or the hope
of the gospel makes men perfect in the sense that their sins
are absolutely forgiven because of the blood of Jesus.

1. Heb. 9:26 - Jesus appeared at the end of the Jewish age
   to put away sin by the sacrifice of Himself.
2. Heb. 10:11-12 - Jesus made one sacrifice for sins forever.
3. Heb. 9:12 - The blood of Jesus obtains eternal redemption for us.
4. Heb. 10:16-18 - Under the New Covenant, sin and iniquities are remembered no more because there is absolute and total forgiveness.

Verses 20-21: *And inasmuch as He was not made priest without*
an oath (for they have become priests without an oath, but He
with an oath by Him who said to Him: "The LORD HAS SWORN
AND WILL NOT RELENT, YOU ARE A PRIEST FOREVER ACCORDING TO THE
ORDER OF MELCHIZEDEK'"), - The Levitical priests were made
priests by virtue of the fact that they descended from Levi
and the family of Aaron, but Christ was made Priest with an
oath. God does not use an oath except to show the certainty and unchanging nature of a promise. In chapter 6:13-18,
the writer had already shown that God swore to Abraham
in order to show the certainty and the unchanging nature of
His promise to him to bless all nations "in Christ." Since this
same assurance which was an oath was given concerning the
priesthood of Christ, the meaning is: God has sworn and will
not change His mind, Christ is going to be a Priest forever.
He will never be replaced by another. The fact that the Levitical priests were made "without an oath" proves that theirs
was not an unchangeable priesthood like the priesthood of
Christ. He does not die, therefore, He will not be succeeded by another. Bear in mind that the writer had already discussed how Christ became a man and how He was tempted
so that He could be a faithful and merciful High Priest (Heb.

2:10-18). **Because He continues as Priest forever, Christians are assured that they will always have a faithful and merciful High Priest who can be touched with human weaknesses. This verse proves that Jesus has a priesthood superior to the Levitical system, because He is faithful and merciful and will never be succeeded by another.**

1. Heb. 2:17 - Jesus was made like His brethren that He might be a merciful and faithful High Priest.
2. Heb. 4:15 - He can be touched with the feeling of our infirmities.
3. Heb. 7:24 - His Priesthood will never be changed or left to another.

Verse 22: *by so much more Jesus has become a surety of a better covenant.* **Because Jesus has been made a priest by an oath of God, He is a guarantee of a better covenant. A superior priest who was made a priest by an oath would demand a superior covenant. The very fact that Jesus became a priest with an oath from God guarantees a better covenant than the first one given by Moses. This theme will be developed in more detail beginning in chapter 8:6ff.**

1. Heb. 7:12 – In this verse it is stated how the law had to be changed because the priesthood had been changed. Knowing that this would create questions in the minds of these Jewish Christians, the writer will discuss in detail the superiority of the new covenant over the old beginning in chapter 8:6 and continuing through chapter 9. Then, in chapter 10 he will show the superiority of the sacrifice of Christ over the sacrifices under the old covenant.
2. The word "better" appears often in the Hebrew letter:
   a. Heb. 1:4 – Christ is *better* than angels.
   b. Heb. 7:19 – Christians have a *better* hope.
   c. Heb. 7:22 – Christians have a *better* covenant.
   d. Heb. 8:6 – Christians have *better* promises.
   e. Heb. 9:23 – Christians have *better* sacrifices.

f.   Heb. 10:34 – Christians have *better* possessions in heaven.

g.   Heb. 11:40 – Christians have a *better* thing
than the OT saints.

h.   Heb. 12:24 – Christians have *better* blood shed
for sins.

Verse 23*: Also there were many priests, because they were prevented by death from continuing.* **Death prevented any one
priest under the old covenant from serving continually, therefore there were many priests who served under that system.
Under the Levitical system there were many priests because
they died and therefore could not continue to serve. Under
that system the people of God might have a good priest today
and a bad one tomorrow. They may have a very sympathic
priest one time and some not so sympathic after he died and
was replaced. They may have a merciful priest one time and
one not so merciful the next.**

1. Isaiah 28:7 - The priests sometimes were drunk and
corrupted justice.
2. Jer. 6:13 - They may deal falsely.
3. Jer. 23:11 - They may be profane.
4. Zechariah 3 - Priests may be good.

Verse 24*: But He, because He continues forever, has an unchangeable priesthood.* **Christ, unlike the priests of the Levitical system, has an unchangeable priesthood. He does not die
and, therefore, He will never be succeeded by another. Bear
in mind that the writer had already discussed how Jesus became a man and how He was tempted in order to be a faithful and merciful High Priest (Heb. 2:14-18). And because He
continues forever, Christians are assured that they will always have a faithful and merciful High Priest ministering for
them.**

1. Heb. 2:17 – He was made like His brethren so He could
be faithful and merciful.

2. Heb. 4:15 – He is affected when we are afflicted.
3. Heb. 7:24 – His priesthood will never be changed or left to another.

Verse 25: *Therefore He is also able to save to the uttermost those who come to God through Him, since He always lives to make intercession for them.*- Because He continues forever as Priest, He is able to save completely those that come to God by Him. He will always be there to take up and intercede for them.

1. Isa. 53:6 - All have gone astray.
2. Matt. 11:28; John 14:6 - All must come to God by Jesus.
3. John 6:44-45 - Men come to Christ by hearing and learning of the Father.

Verse 26: *For such a High Priest was fitting for us, who is holy, harmless, undefiled, separate from sinners, and has become higher than the heavens;* - It was only fitting and necessary for us to have a sinless priest who is the sinless Son of God.

1. Holy - God-like, pious, devout.
2. Harmless - without ill will.
3. Undefiled - without sin, without spot.
4. Separate from sinners - He was separate from sinners while on earth, because He did not sin (Heb. 4:15). He is now in heaven where sinners cannot go.
5. Made higher than the heavens - exalted above all.

Verse 27: *who does not need daily, as those high priests, to offer up sacrifices, first for His own sins and then for the people's, for this He did once for all when He offered up Himself.* - Christ does not have to offer sacrifices daily for His own sins and then for those of His people like Levitical priests. Why? Because He offered Himself as a sacrifice once for all time to provide forgiveness for the people.

1. Heb. 9:7 - The high priest under the Levitical system had to offer for his own sins and then for the sins of the people.
2. John 10:18 - Christ offered Himself.
3. Heb. 9:26 - He sacrificed Himself.
4. "Once" means once for all time, never to be offered again. The same word is used in Hebrews 9:28 and Jude 1:3.

Verse 28: *For the law appoints as high priests men who have weakness,-* The law made men high priests who had weaknesses and were themselves subject to fall into all kind of sin.

1. Numbers 20:7-12 - Aaron, after his appointment to the office of high priest, was guilty of sin on this occasion, along with Moses. This shows just how weak the high priests were.
2. John 18:13; Matt. 26:57-68 - Caiaphas was a wicked high priest.

but the word of the oath, which came after - The word of oath recorded in Psalms 110:4 was given a long time after the law was given by Moses. God spoke the oath through David and he was the second king of Israel. The law was given to Israel at Mount Sinai, then there was the wandering in the wilderness, the period of the judges, the reign of Saul (the first king), and then the reign of David. Therefore it had been a long time since the law was given when the word of oath was made through David in the Psalms.

appoints the Son who has been perfected forever. - The appointment of Christ is complete and permanent. He has been perfected for evermore.

SPECIAL NOTE: Thus far in the Book of Hebrews, the writer has shown that *Jesus is a superior High Priest* to those of the Levitical system by pointing out the following things:

1. Heb. 4:14 - He is the Son of God.
2. Heb. 4:15 - He is without sin.
3. Heb. 5:6 - He is of a higher order than the Levitical priesthood.
4. Heb. 5:9 - He obtained eternal salvation (Aaron only temporary).
5. Heb. 5:9 - He obtained salvation for all who would obey (Aaron Israel only).
6. Heb. 7:20-21, 28 - He was made priest with an oath.
7. Heb. 7:24 - He has an unchangeable Priesthood.
8. Heb. 7:25 - He lives forever to make intercession.
9. Heb. 7:26 - He is holy, harmless, undefiled, separate from sinners, and made higher than the heavens.
10. Heb. 7:27 - He has offered a greater sacrifice - Himself.

HEBREWS
Chapter Eight

JESUS IS THE MEDIATOR OF
A SUPERIOR COVENANT

SPECIAL NOTE: In chapter 8, the writer continues his discussion of the superior priesthood of Christ. Beginning in verse 6 of this chapter, he will begin showing that the New Covenant is superior to the Old Covenant. This fact would continue to show that the Priesthood of Christ is superior to the Levitical system, because it would show that *Jesus is a Priest over a superior covenant* to that of the Levitical priests. In Hebrews 7:22 the writer had stated that Jesus is the "*surety of a better covenant.*" In this chapter he will say more about this better Covenant and show that it was predicted by Jeremiah while the Old Covenant was still in force. He will state that Jesus is the "Mediator" and that it contains *better promises.* Therefore it is *superior to the old one* and the old one was about to vanish away completely.

Verse 1: *Now this is the main point of the things we are saying* - Everything the writer has said, concerning the priesthood, builds up to this one great point.

We have such a High Priest - That is, we have such a High Priest as he has been discussing in the preceding chapters.

1. Heb. 2:17 - He is faithful and merciful.
2. Heb. 2:18 – He is able to aid those who are tempted.
3. Heb. 4:14 – He is the Son of God.
4. Heb. 4:15 - He is without sin.
5. Heb. 5:9 - He obtained eternal salvation for all.
6. Heb. 5:10 - He is called a high priest according to the

order of Melchizedek.
7. Heb. 7:20-21 - He is made priest with an oath.
8. Heb. 7:24 - He has an unchangeable priesthood.
9. Heb. 7:25 - He lives forever to make intercession for us.
10. Heb. 7:26 - He is holy, harmless, undefiled, separa from sinners, and made higher than the heavens.
11. Heb. 7:27 - He offered Himself as a sacrifice.

who is seated at the right hand of the throne of the Majesty in the heavens - Christ, the High Priest under the New Covenant, is seated at the right hand of God in heaven.

1. Heb. 10:11-12 - This proves that the right hand of the Majesty is the right hand of God.
2. Heb. 10:11-12 - He sat down on the right hand of God after He had offered Himself as a sacrifice for sins.
3. Heb. 9:24 - He has entered into heaven itself. He has entered into heaven itself to appear in the presence of God for us.

Verse 2: *a Minister of the sanctuary* - The sanctuary in which Christ ministers on behalf of His people is heaven itself.

1. Heb. 9:24 - Christ ministers for us in "heaven itself."
2. Heb. 6:19-20 – He is the forerunner of us.

and of the true tabernacle - This must refer to the church. There are some who think that "sanctuary" and "tabernacle" refer to the same thing. However, the words "and of" indicate that there is a difference between the two. The high priest, during the Old Testament period, ministered in both the holy place (which was a type of the church) and the most holy place (which was a type of heaven). In a similar manner, Christ ministers in both the church and in heaven.

which the Lord erected, and not man - Moses and the Israelites built the tabernacle in the Old Testament. Christ, however, built the true tabernacle or the church.

1. Exodus 25-40 - These chapters record the building of the tabernacle by Moses and the Israelites.
2. Matt. 16:18 - Jesus built the church.

Verse 3: *For every high priest is appointed to offer both gifts and sacrifices* - Those high priests under the Levitical system were appointed to offer gifts and sacrifices for sins.

1. Heb. 5:1 - They were to offer both gifts and sacrifices for sins.
2. Heb. 9:7 – He offered for his sins and also for the sins of the people.

Therefore it is necessary that this One also have something to offer - Since Christ is the Christian's High Priest, He had to have something to offer for sins. What He offered has already been stated by the writer in chapter 7:27 - Himself.

1. Heb. 9:12 - He offered His own blood.
2. Heb. 9:26 - He sacrificed Himself.
3. Heb. 9:28 - He offered Himself to bear the sins of many.
4. Heb. 9:28 - He offered Himself once for all.

Verse 4: *For if He were on earth, He would not be a priest* - Since Christ was not of the tribe of Levi and the house of Aaron, He could not be a priest while He was on earth.

1. Heb. 7:14 - Jesus was of the tribe of Judah.
2. Heb. 7:13 - No man of the tribe of Judah ever served as priest.

since there are priests who offer the gifts according to the law - The Law of Moses required that certain gifts be offered by the high priest for sin.

Verse 5: *who serve the copy and shadow of the heavenly things*
- The Old Testament, with its ordinances and priests, pictured or foreshadowed the priesthood to come.

    1. Heb. 10:1 - The law served as a shadow of good things
        to come.
    2. Heb. 9:9-11 – The offerings of the OT were symbolic
        of things to come.

*as Moses was divinely instructed when he was about to make
the tabernacle. For He said, See that you make all things according to the pattern shown you on the mountain* - Moses
was not allowed to add to or take from the pattern that God
showed him for the tabernacle. The tabernacle was a shadow
or type of something to come in the Christian Age. Because
God knew that the tabernacle was to be a type of things in the
New Testament, He instructed Moses to make it according to
the divine pattern.

    1. Ex. 25:40 - God told Moses to make the tabernacle ac-
        cording to the pattern.
    2. Heb. 9 - The writer will discuss the tabernacle more
        fully in this chapter.

SPECIAL NOTE: Beginning in chapter 8:6 and continuing
through chapter 9, Paul will discuss the superiority of the
New Covenant over the Old. He had already mentioned the
fact that the law had to be changed (7:12) and that Jesus is
a guarantee of a better covenant (7:22). He now proceeds to
show that this New Covenant is superior to the old one. At
the same time, he will show the Jewish Christians that God
had foretold this change in covenants in the Old Testament
Scriptures (Heb. 8:8-12).

Verse 6: *But now He has obtained a more excellent ministry*
- Christ has obtained a more excellent ministry than that under the Levitical system. He ministers under a New Covenant. He ministers in a higher place - in heaven and in the

very presence of God Himself. Therefore, He has obtained a more excellent ministry.

inasmuch as He is also Mediator of a better covenant - Jesus is the mediator of a better covenant because He is the covenant that God has made with man.

1. Heb. 7:22 - A superior priest demands a better covenant and the writer has already stated this fact.
2. Gal. 3:19; Deut. 5:5 - Moses was the mediator of the Old Testament. He stood between God and Israel.
3. A mediator is a go-between. The Old Testament high priest was one who stood between God and man.
4. Heb. 12:24 - Jesus is the mediator of the New Covenant. He stands between God and man.
5. 1 Tim. 2:5 - Jesus is the only mediator between God and man.

which was established on better promises - The New Covenant has superior promises to those in the Old Covenant. This shows that the "New" is superior to the "Old" because of the promises it contains. What are some of those better promises?

1.   Heb. 8:12 - Absolute forgiveness of sin.
2.   Heb. 11:39-40 - The coming of Christ.
3.   Eph. 1:3 - All spiritual blessings.
4.   Acts 2:38, 39 - The gift of the Holy Spirit.
5.   John 14:1 - The promise of mansions in heaven.
6.   2 Pet. 3:18 - Life in the new heavens and new earth.
7.   1 John 2:25 - The promise of eternal life.
8.   Heb. 11:40 - God has provided something better for us who are in Christ.

Verse 7: *For if that first covenant had been faultless, then no place would have been sought for a second* - The meaning is, if the Law of Moses (first covenant) had been faultless, then there would have been no need for a second covenant (the gospel). The word faultless does not mean that there were mistakes in the first covenant. The fault was in the fact that the Law of Moses could not give life, because no one could keep it perfectly. If the Law of Moses had been sufficient to accomplish God's complete purpose for man's salvation, then there would have been no need for a second covenant. If the Law of Moses could have given absolute forgiveness, then there would have been no need of seeking a second covenant.

1. Gal. 3:21 - The Old Law couldn't give life, because the people could not keep it perfectly.
2. Heb. 10:4 - The sacrifices could not take away sin.
3. Heb. 7:11 - There was no perfection or total forgiveness in the absolute forgiveness.

Verse 8: *Because finding fault with them* - God found fault with the people of the first covenant. The people did not continue in all things demanded in the covenant. The history of Israel shows that they could not and did not do what the law required.

He says - The following is a quotation from Jeremiah 31:31-34.

Behold, the days are coming, says the LORD, when I will make a new covenant with the house of Israel and with the house of Judah - Jeremiah wrote after the kingdom of Israel had been divided. The Northern Kingdom of Israel and the Southern Kingdom of Judah would be included in the New Covenant.

Verse 9: *not according to the covenant that I made with their fathers in the day when I took them by the hand to lead them out of the land of Egypt* - The "covenant made with their fathers" refers to the Law of Moses, which was given exclusively to Israel. The phrase "in the day" is used metaphorically (a phrase used in the place of another to denote a likeness between them) for the period in which God led them out of Egypt.

1. Deut. 5:1-3 - The Law of Moses was given to Israel.
2. Gal. 5:1-5 – The law was a yoke of bondage that none could keep.

because they did not continue in My covenant - The Israelites had agreed to do what God said, but they failed to keep their part of the agreement. They failed to obey all of the things God told them to do.

1. Ex. 19:8; 24:3, 7 - The Israelites agreed to do what Jehovah said.
2. Jeremiah 11:6-8 - The Israelites did not obey God.
3. The dictionary will define a "covenant" as a binding formal agreement or promise usually under seal between two or more parties.

and I disregarded them, says the Lord - That is, God treated them as an unfaithful people. He rejected them because they did not keep their part of the agreement.

Verse 10: *For this is the covenant that I will make with the house of Israel after those days, says the LORD: I will put My laws in their mind and write them on their hearts* - Some in the Old Testament treasured the word and kept it in their hearts. There were devout Jews such as Moses, David and numerous others. The great majority, however, never really received God's law into their hearts. Therefore, to them it was always a letter inscribed on stone and not an indwelling power in the heart. However, under the New Covenant, a person must receive the word into his heart before he can enter into this covenant relationship with God (Jas. 1:21; Lk. 8:5-18). That is, they must receive Jesus into their hearts in order to enter the covenant with God (Col. 2:6-12). Once He is received as *Lord*, He begins writing His will or laws in their hearts by His indwelling presence and Spirit.

1. Rom. 8:14 – God leads those who are born again and

thereby enter the new covenant by means of His Spirit.
2. 2 Pet. 1:20-21; 2 Tim. 3:16-17 - Jesus also writes His laws in our hearts by means of the words He taught us in the Scriptures.

and I will be their God, and they shall be My people - God is, to those who enter the New Covenant by the new birth, their God in an even higher sense than He was to those faithful Jews under the Old Covenant. They have Jesus, who is the covenant, dwelling in their hearts and that is why they are Christians.

1. Gal. 4:6 - Christians are sons and they belong to Jesus who belongs to God. Hence, He is our God in a very special way.
2. 1 John 3:1 - Christians are sons of God in a very special sense.
3. Gal. 3:26-29 – We are in Christ and we have put on Christ and are at that point in the covenant.
4. Isaiah 42:6; 49:8 – Jesus is the new covenant God was going to make with His people.

Verse 11: *None of them shall teach his neighbor, and none his brother, saying, Know the LORD* - Under the Old Covenant, men were born as members of the covenant. Later, when those children were old enough to understand, they were then taught to "know the Lord."

for all shall know Me, from the least of them to the greatest of them - In the New Covenant, unlike the Old Covenant, a person must know the Lord or receive Jesus as Lord (Col. 2:6) in order to enter the new covenant relationship with God. In the New Covenant, all know Him from the least (babe/immature) to the greatest (mature/full grown).

1. John 6:44, 45 - Men must be taught of God before they can be members of the New Covenant.
2. Therefore we must know and receive Jesus as Lord or

know the Lord before they can become members.

Verse 12: *For I will be merciful to their unrighteousness, and their sins and their lawless deeds I will remember no more* - Under the New Covenant, there is absolute forgiveness of sins. The sins forgiven under the New Covenant are "remembered no more."

1. Heb. 10:3 - During the Levitical system there was a remembrance made of sins by the sacrifices offered.
2. Jn. 1:29 - Under the New Testament, sins are remembered no more because the Lamb of God has taken them away completely and permanently. Therefore, the New Covenant is far superior to the Old.

SPECIAL NOTE: This quotation from Jeremiah would serve to show the Jewish Christians that God, even in Old Covenant times, had planned to change from the Old Covenant to something better. Therefore, when the Judaizing teachers came to them and said, "Look, we have the priesthood, the temple, and the Old Testament." The Hebrew Christian could say, "Yes, and even in the Old Testament we were foretold that God was one day going to make a new and better covenant with His people, which He has now done in Christ."

Verse 13: *In that He says, A new covenant, He has made the first obsolete. Now what is becoming obsolete and growing old is ready to vanish away* - Here the writer says that the Old Covenant system was ready to vanish away. But someone objects, saying, "I thought the Old Covenant Law ended at the cross. How can the writer now say that it is *ready* to vanish away?"

The answer to this objection is, "As far as God was concerned, and as far as the Law of Moses being God's law for man, it did end at the cross. The law actually ended at that time, but God allowed them to continue with the sacrifices, temple, and priesthood until Jerusalem fell in 70 A.D. At that time, the Old Testament system vanished away completely in every sense of the word. The Levitical systems can never be restored as it was during Old Testament times because the re-cords, genealogies, sacrifices, and Temple were all complete-ly and permanently destroyed forever by the Romans when they destroyed Jerusalem and the temple in 70 A.D.

HEBREWS
Chapter Nine

JESUS MINISTERS IN A SUPERIOR TABERNACLE

SPECIAL NOTE: In this chapter, the writer continues to discuss the superiority of the New Covenant over the Old. He began showing this in chapter 8:6, and he continues throughout this chapter. In chapter 8:5, he had mentioned the fact that the Old Covenant services were designed as shadows and types of things to come or heavenly things. He mentioned specifically the tabernacle, and, in this present chapter, he is going to show that the earthly tabernacle was only a shadow, or type, of something to come. He will then show that the antitype is superior to the type. Or to put it another way, the things which the tabernacle typified are superior to the tabernacle and its service. Therefore, *Jesus ministers in a tabernacle (heaven) that is far superior to the old one.* Beginning in verse 23 of this chapter, the writer will begin showing that the sacrifices of the New Testament are superior to those offered in the Old.

Verse 1: *Then indeed, even the first covenant* - This refers to the Old Covenant and all of the Law of Moses.

1. Heb. 8:13 - The first covenant is the Old Covenant.
2. Heb. 10:9-10 - Christ took away the first (old) covenant in order to establish the second (new) covenant.

had ordinances of divine service - The emphasis here is on the fact that the first covenant had rules and laws of service that were given by God. They were divinely ordained by God.

1. Heb. 8:5 - God gave Moses the pattern for the tabernacle.

    2. Neh. 8:14 - God gave the commandments through Moses regarding the Old Covenant with the various services and sacrifices.

and the earthly sanctuary - It was a sanctuary of this world or earthly sanctuary when compared to the church and heaven which are spiritual in nature.

    1. Ex. 25:8-27:21 - The Old Covenant sanctuary or holy place where God dwells in a special way was built by the Israelites, and built from materials of this earth such as wood, gold, staves, etc.
    2. John 18:36; Matt. 16:18 - The church, however, is not of this world - that is, it is a spiritual temple and it was built by Jesus.

Verse 2: *For a tabernacle was prepared* - The tabernacle was the first sanctuary or place where God would manifest Himself in a special way.

    1. The tabernacle was to Israel what a Church building is to many religious people today.
    2. Ex. 25:8-9 - It was the place where God would dwell among them.
    3. Ex. 25:40; Heb. 8:5 - God gave Moses the pattern for it when Moses was on Mount Sinai. It was to serve as a type or shadow of things in the New Testament and that is why God gave the pattern.

the first part - This must refer to the "first compartment" of the tabernacle.
There were two compartments in the tabernacle which were the Holy Place and the Most Holy Place, or the Holy of Holies. The next statement shows that the writer refers to the first compartment, because he says, "In which was the lamp stand, etc.?" The lamp stand as well as the table and the showbread were in the first compartment of the tabernacle

in which was the lamp stand - In the first compartment of the tabernacle there was a lamp stand.

1. Ex. 37:17-24 - This is the description of the lamp stand.
2. Ex. 40:24; 26:35 - The lamp stand was on the south side of the tabernacle.

the table, and the showbread, which is called the sanctuary - The table of showbread was also in the Holy Place or the first section of the tabernacle. On this table, the priest placed twelve cakes - six in a row - and they were eaten by the priests.

1. Lev. 24:5-9 - The bread was eaten by the priests.
2. Ex. 40:22 - The table was on the north side of the tabernacle.

SPECIAL NOTE: In this first compartment was also the altar of incense. I don't know why the writer did not mention it here, but it was in the Holy Place along with the lamp stand and table of showbread.

1. Ex. 30:1-10 - The priest burned incense on it every morning and evening.
2. Ex. 40:26-27 - These verses show that it was in the Holy Place, and also that the priests burned incense on it.
3. Ex. 40:26 - The golden altar (altar of incense) was placed in front of the veil or the large curtain that separated the Holy Place from the Most Holy Place.
4. Some suggest that it may have been used both in the Holy Place and also in the Most Holy Place.
5. Heb. 9:5 - The statement "of which we cannot now speak in detail" seems to indicate that it was not his purpose to discuss the tabernacle system of worship in detail at this time. This may be why he did not mention the "altar of incense" as being part of the furniture in the Holy Place.

Verse 3: *and behind the second veil* - The first veil or large curtain was at the entrance to the tabernacle. The second veil or large curtain was used to separate the Holy Place from the Most Holy Place and was, therefore, in actuality the "second veil."

1. Ex. 26:33 - The second veil divided the Holy Place from the Most Holy Place.
2. Matt. 27:51 - This second veil is the one that was torn from top to bottom when Christ died on the cross.

the part of the tabernacle which is called the Holiest of All - The second compartment of the tabernacle was called the Holy of Holies, the Most Holy Place, or the Holiest of All.

which had the golden censer - A censer is a vessel used for the burning of incense (Lev. 16:12, 13). There has been some controversy over how this Greek phrase should be translated whether "altar of incense" or "golden censer." The A.S.V. renders this as the "altar of incense," and if that is the case we have already explained what this means in the comments on verse 2. Some have said otherwise and thought that the rendering should be "golden censer" and not "altar of incense." The NKJV that I use renders it "golden censer." Berry, Green, Young, and the Living Oracles support "golden censer." Robert Milligan in his commentary on Hebrews said the evidence is on the side of "golden censer." Who knows?

and the ark of the covenant overlaid on all sides with gold - This was the chest-like object that contained the two tables of the covenant. Hence, it was called the Ark of the Covenant, because it was the ark that contained the covenant.

1. Deut. 10:1-5 - Moses put the two tables of stone in the ark he had made.
2. Ex. 37:1-9 - These verses give the description of the Ark of the Covenant.

in which were the golden pot that had the manna - This refers to the pot that had manna in it and it was kept in the Ark of the Covenant to remind the Israelites of the fact that God fed them with manna for forty years.

1. Ex. 16:33-35 — These verses record the manna being put and kept before the testimony or in the Ark of the Covenant.
2. Ex. 16:31 - Manna was something like a wafer made with honey.

Aaron's rod that budded - This refers to the rod of Aaron that budded, bloomed, blossomed, and even brought forth almonds. It was kept in the Ark of the Covenant as a sign of the authority of Moses and the family of Aaron.

1. Num. 16 - Several rebelled against the authority of Moses and Aaron.
2. Num. 17:1-9 - The budding of Aaron's rod was brought about by rebellion and served to show who God had selected as priests.
3. Num. 17:10 - The rod of Aaron was placed in the ark and kept as a token of the authority of Aaron.

and the tablets of the covenant - This refers to the two tablets of stone on which God wrote the Ten Commandments, which were the basis, or foundation, for the entire Mosaic Law. The two tablets were placed in the Ark of the Covenant.

1. Deut. 10:1-5 - These verses record the placing of the two tables of stone in the ark.
2. Deut. 4:12-13 - God first spoke the Ten Commandments to Israel and later wrote them on two tablets of stone.
3. Deut. 9:11 - The two tablets of stone are called the "tablets of the covenant" because they were the basis or foundation for all of the laws given by Moses.

Verse 5: *and above it were the cherubim of glory overshadowing the mercy seat -*   Above the ark were Cherubim which seem to be an order of angels. They represented the glory of the Lord overshadowing the ark.

    1. Ex. 25:17-22 - These verses describe the Cherubims. They seem to resemble angels and they had wings. There were two of them, one on each end of the ark, facing each other. This may have represented the presence of angels in the Most Holy Place.
    2. Gen. 3:24 - This indicates these Cherubims were an order of angels.

Of these things we cannot now speak in detail - This seems to mean that the writer could not discuss these things in detail "now" or at that particular time. It was not his purpose in the letter and he didn't have time to go into it in any depth.

SPECIAL STUDY: The tabernacle was a shadow of things to come in the Christian Age. With this in mind, a very profitable study would be to see what each item involved in the tabernacle system of worship might foreshadow or represent in the Christian Age.

   I.   In the Court of the Tabernacle there was:

   1. The Altar of Burnt Offerings

      a. Ex. 27:1-8 - This is the description of the altar.
      b. Ex. 40:29 - It was located in the court and it was close to the entrance into the court. The court surrounded the tabernacle itself.
      c. Ex. 40:29 - On this altar, the sacrifices for sins were offered.
      d. Heb. 13:10-12 – In the new covenant we have an altar and it is the sacrifice of Christ for our sins.
      e. Heb. 9:26 - Jesus sacrificed Himself as an offering for sin.

2. The Laver

    a. Ex. 40:7, 30 - The laver was also placed in the court, between the altar of burnt offerings and the tabernacle.

    b. The laver was a vessel of brass with water in it for the priests to wash their hands and feet.

    c. Ex. 30:17-21 - The priests washed before entering the tabernacle in the water in the laver.

    d. Note: In the New Testament we also must be washed in water before we enter the church of Christ. The Holy Place in the tabernacle was a type of the Church in the New Testament. As the priest had to come by the altar of burnt offerings, and wash in the laver before entering into the Holy Place, just so, must men today go by the altar or the sacrifice of Christ and be born of water or baptized in water and the Spirit before they enter the church of Christ.

    e. Titus 3:5; John 3:5 - Men must be "born of water" to enter the kingdom.

    f. Heb. 10:22; Eph. 5:26 - They must have their bodies washed with the washing of water by the word.

I.   In the Holy Place of the Tabernacle which was a type of the New Testament church there was:

1. The Lampstand

    a. Ex. 37:17-24 - It provided the light in the Holy Place for the priests.

    b. Ex. 40:24 - It was located in the Holy Place of the tabernacle, and was the only light for the room,

    c. Note: In the New Testament Church, we too have a lamp and light. The lamp stand was a type of the word of God. In Psalm 119:105 we learn that the word of God is a "lamp" and "light."

2. **The Table of Showbread.**

    a. **Lev. 24:5-9** - The bread on this table was eaten on the Sabbath Day by the priests, after they had been by the altar of burnt offerings and the laver.

    b. **Exodus 40:22** – It was located in the Holy Place of the tabernacle.

    c. **NOTE:** In the New Testament Church the Lord's Supper is generally eaten by New Testament priests on the first day of every week. The table of showbread was a type of the Lord's Supper. Only after going by the sacrifice of Christ, and by the laver of baptism are men to eat the Lord's Supper.

    d. **Matt. 26:24** - The Lord's Supper is to be eaten in the kingdom or in the church.

    e. **Acts 20:7** – In the church at Troas they met on the first day of the week to break bread.

    f. **1 Peter 2:9; Rev. 1:6** - All Christians are priests in the New Testament Church and they are the ones who have the privilege of eating the Supper.

3. **The Altar of Incense**

    a. **Ex. 40:26, 27** - It was also located in the Holy Place of the tabernacle.

    b. **Ex. 30:1-10** - The priests burned incense on it every morning and evening. This item stood before the veil in front of the Most Holy Place, so that, when the incense was burned, the fragrance penetrated the veil and permeated the Most Holy Place.

    c. **NOTE:** In the church, the incense is the prayers of the saints. The incense offered on the altar of incense was a type of the prayers of the Christian priests.

    d. **Rev. 5:8** - The incense offered in the New Testament are the "prayers of the saints."

e. Matt. 6:9 – Prayers of believers penetrate
into heaven, just like the incense penetrated into the Most
Holy Place.

II.   The Most Holy Place in the Tabernacle was a type of
      Heaven in the New Testament.

As the High Priest went through the Holy Place to get to the
Most Holy Place, so all men must come through the church or
New Covenant "Holy Place" in order to get to heaven or the
New Covenant "Most Holy Place".

Special Note concerning the Old Testament Tabernacle:
During the days of David, he realized that the ark of God
dwelled in curtains or in the tabernacle (2 Sam: 7:1-6) and he
desired to build God a permanent house in Jerusalem. David,
however, was not allowed to build the house because he was
a man of war (1 Kings 5:3; 1 Chron. 28:2-3). Thus, Solomon
was appointed to build the house of the Lord or the temple in
Jerusalem (1 Chron. 28:6, 7; 1 Kings 6:1-38). The Tabernacle was replaced by the more permanent Temple and yet the
types and shadows remained the same.

Verse 6: *Now when these things had been thus prepared* –
When these things were appointed like they were the priests
served in the Tabernacle.

*the priests always went into the first part of the tabernacle per-
forming the services* - The first compartment or section of
the tabernacle was the Holy Place. This refers to the common priests who performed their duties in the Holy Place of
the Tabernacle, and were not allowed to enter the Most Holy
Place.

1. Ex. 30:7, 8 - They burned incense in the Holy Place
   every morning and evening.
2. They dressed and lit lamps at evening. This was likely
   not all they did but it was part of it.

3. Lk. 1:5-12 – This is where Zacharias, the father of John the Baptist, was when the angel appeared to him.
4. There was only one high priest at a time.
   However, there were many common priests. All the priests came from the tribe of Levi and the family of Aaron. All the priests were Levites, but not all the Levites were priests. Only those Levites who were of the family of Aaron served as priests.

Verse 7: *But into the second part the high priest went alone:* The High Priest was the only one allowed to go into the Most Holy Place.

1. Lev. 16 - This chapter explains his going into the Most Holy Place.
2. Heb. 5:1 – The High Priest was appointed for men in regard to things spiritual, such as gifts and sacrifices for sin.

once a year - The High Priest was the only one who could go into the Most Holy Place, and he only went in one time per year.

1. Lev. 23:27 - The tenth day of the seventh month was the Day of Atonement which some think was our September or October. On this day, he went into the Most Holy Place at least three times. The statement "once a year" does not mean only one time, but only on one day.
2. He went in at least two times on that one day:
   a. Lev. 16:12-14- To carry the coals and sweet incense into the Most Holy Place and carry the blood of the bull to sprinkle it on and before the mercy seat.
   b. Lev. 16:15 - To carry the blood of a goat and do as he had done with the blood of the bullock.

not without blood, which he offered for himself and for the people's sins committed in ignorance - The statement "not without blood" meant that he had to carry blood on this day to make atonement for himself and for the sins of the people. These sins were not sins of high handed rebellion but ignorance.

1. Heb. 7:27 - He had to offer an offering first for his own sins, and then for those of the people.
2. Lev. 16:11-14 - The blood of the calf was offered for the sins of the High Priest.
3. Lev. 16:15, 46 - The blood of the goat was for the sins of the people.
4. Heb. 9:25 - He took the blood of others like goats and calves, but not his own.
5. The sins here were involuntary. This includes all sins, except those which were committed in open defiance and contempt for God's law. For such sins there was no sacrifice offered (Num. 15:30-31).

Verse 8: *the Holy Spirit indicating this, that the way into the Holiest of All was not yet made manifest, while the first tabernacle was still standing* - The fact that no one but the High Priest was allowed to go behind the veil served to demonstrate that the way to heaven—which was the anti-type of the Most Holy Place of the Tabernacle was still a mystery or a matter not fully revealed or understood by anyone, except God Himself, while the Tabernacle and Temple worship continued with God's approval.

1. Only Christ's death revealed the ultimate purpose of God.
2. Matt. 27:51 - When Christ died on the cross, the "veil of the temple was torn in two from the top to the bottom" and that signified that the way to heaven (the anti-type of the Most Holy Place) is now made known by the blood of Christ. However, the way to heaven by the blood of Christ was not made known

while Tabernacle/Temple worship was in force.

3. 1 Cor. 2:7-10 - During the times before the gospel, it had not entered the heart of man the things God had prepared for those who love Him.

4. Eph. 3:3-6 - In others ages (Patriarchal/Mosaic), the gospel or the mystery (sacred secret) was not made known as it is now.

Verse 9: *It was symbolic for the present time* - The Tabernacle system of worship was only designed to be temporary and served as a figure, type, and shadow of things to come. One reason the writer brought up the Tabernacle was to show that it was only a figure, type, and shadow of something that was to come. Why should these Hebrew believers leave the substance and go back to the shadow?

in which both gifts and sacrifices are offered which cannot make him who performed the service perfect in regard to the conscience - The gifts and sacrifices, offered under the Tabernacle system of worship, were not able to clear the conscience of the worshipper. The sacrifices offered reminded men of sin, but did not cleanse the conscience. The sacrifices of the Old Testament did not make the worshipper conscious of the fact that his sins had been absolutely forgiven. The sacrifices obtained a good standing for them during the time the Tabernacle system was in force, but nothing more.

1. Heb. 10:3, 4 - The sacrifices offered did not take away their sins.

2. Heb. 10:1 - The sacrifices which they offered could not make them perfect or forgiven in the absolute sense.

3. Heb. 7:19 - The law made nothing perfect.

Verse 10: *concerned only with foods and drinks, various washings, and fleshly ordinances* – These were rules that pertained to the flesh. The writer's point is that man's conscience could not be cleared with these gifts and sacrifices since they were composed of foods and drinks and pertained to the flesh and not to the heart of man.

1. Ex. 29:40-41 - There were drink offerings.
2. Lev. 16:4, 24 - The "washings" may refer to the washing the priest did on the Day of Atonement before entering the tabernacle.

imposed until the time of reformation - This shows that the Law of Moses was to last only until the time of reformation.

1. The "time of reformation" refers to the time of Christ and the New Covenant.
2. Gal. 3:19 - The Law of Moses was to last until the seed (Christ) should come.

Verse 11: *But Christ came as High Priest of the good things to come* - Christ is the antitype of the Old Testament high priest. He is the High Priest of good things to come. He is the High Priest over the system to which the Old Testament High Priest was pointing.

1. Heb. 10:1 - The law was a shadow of good things to come and Christ is the High Priest of good things to come. This shows that the Tabernacle worship was no longer operative because the "good things to come"' were already here.
2. The Judaizers could say, "We have the temple worship." Then the Christian could answer, "Yes, but that was only to last until the time of reformation."

with the greater and more perfect tabernacle - He had just described the tabernacle worship (9:1-9), and said that it was only to last until the reformation (v. 10). Now he begins to show the superiority of Christ's ministry over the ministry of the Old Testament high priests. The Old Testament high priests ministered in a tabernacle made with hands, while Christ ministers in heaven on behalf of the church. The Old Testament tabernacle was a worldly sanctuary (Heb. 9:1).

1. Heb. 9:24 - Christ ministers in heaven itself.
2. Heb. 4:14 - Christ has passed into the heavens.
3. Heb. 3:6 - Christ is High Priest over a spiritual house.

not made with hands, that is, not of this creation - The Old Testament tabernacle was made with human hands out of earthly material. However, Christ is in heaven (a spiritual place) and ministers on behalf of the church (a spiritual kingdom).

1. 2 Cor. 5:1 - Heaven is a spiritual place where we will need a spiritual body or a body not made with hands.
2. Dan. 2:34 – The stone, representing the church or kingdom, was "cut out without hands". Therefore it is a spiritual kingdom.
3. John 18:36 - Christ's kingdom is not of this world.

Verse 12: *Not with the blood of goats and calves* - This refers to the blood of the animals that the Old Testament high priest offered on the Day of Atonement.

1. Lev. 16:6 - The High Priest offered the blood of a calf for his own sins and those of his house.
2. Lev. 16:15 - The blood of a goat was offered for the sins of the people.

but with His own blood - Christ did not use the blood of goats and calves like the Old Testament high priests, but rather, He offered His own blood for the sins of the people.

1. Matt. 26:28 - This verse tells what remits sins, while Acts 2:38 deals with when they are remitted.
2. Rev. 1:5 - This verse tells what washes away sins, while Acts 22:16 deals with when they are washed away.
3. 1 Peter 1:18, 19 - In these verses, Peter tells us what redeems us, and in the same book he deals with when we are redeemed (1 Peter 3:21).

4. Heb. 9:14 - This verse tells what purges the conscience and 1 Peter 3:21 deals with when the conscience is purged.

He entered the Most Holy Place – He entered heaven which is the true or real Most Holy Place.

1. Heb. 9:24 - Here the writer clearly shows that Christ entered heaven itself.
2. Heb. 8:12 - Under Christ and the New Covenant sins are "remembered no more."

once for all having obtained eternal redemption - The word once refers once for all time. It is eternal redemption or redemption that lasts forever.

1. Heb. 9:26 - Once at the end of the Jewish age He appeared to put away sin by the sacrifice of Himself.
2. Heb. 9:28 - Christ was offered one time for all time to bear the sins of many.

Verse 13: *For if the blood of bulls and goats* - This refers to the animals offered on the Day of Atonement. The blood made atonement for the soul because God said it would (Lev. 17:11).

and the ashes of a heifer, sprinkling the unclean - This refers to the ashes of a red heifer that had to be sprinkled on those who were ceremonially unclean.

1. Numbers 19:1-22 - This chapter records the law concerning the ashes of the heifer. The red heifer was burned and the ashes were put in water then sprinkled on the people for ceremonial cleansing.
2. This was done to those who had touched a dead body, or those who came into a tent where a dead man was.

sanctifies for the purifying of the flesh - That is, they cleansed a person outwardly or ceremonially. These Jewish Christians would agree that the blood of goats and calves and the ashes of a heifer cleansed men ceremonially, because God had said it would. If a person had touched a dead body and had the ashes of a heifer sprinkled on him, then after a certain time all devout Jews would admit that he was clean.

Verse 14: *how much more shall the blood of Christ* - If they admit that the blood of goats and calves and the ashes of a heifer cleansed because God said it would, then how much more should the blood of Christ purge men from sin. All Jews would admit that the blood of animals had some value, and if so, how much more value should the blood of Christ have.

who through the eternal Spirit - It was through the direction of and by the power of the Holy Spirit that Christ offered Himself without spot to God.

1. 1 Peter 3:18 - Christ was raised from the dead by the power of the Holy Spirit.
2. Some think that the eternal Spirit refers to Christ's own eternal Spirit and not the Holy Spirit.
3. If I am right in thinking that it refers to the Holy Spirit, then this is another verse that teaches that the Holy Spirit is just as eternal as the Father and Son.

offered Himself without spot to God - Christ offered Himself "without spot to God" which means that He offered Himself as a sinless sacrifice for sin.

1. 1 Peter 1:19 - Christ offered Himself as a Lamb without blemish and without spot.
2. John 10:17-18 - He laid down His own life.
3. Heb. 7:27 - He offered up Himself.
4. Heb. 4:15 - He was without spot or sin.
5. Lev. 1:10; 22:19-22 - The Old Testament sacrifices had to be without spot or blemish.

cleanse your conscience from dead works to serve the living God? – The writer had already said that the blood of animals could not give them a clear conscience (Heb. 9:9), because there was no absolute forgiveness (Heb. 10:4). He now points out that the blood of Christ does cleanse the conscience from works that lead to death and causes men to serve the living God.

1. Heb. 8:12 - The blood of Christ cleanses our conscience because it provides absolute forgiveness.
2. Heb. 6:1-2 – The writer had already referred to "dead works" here.
3. Matt. 25:14-30 - The parable of the talents teaches that Christians who refuse to serve will not be saved.

Verse 15: *And for this reason He is the Mediator of the new covenant* - Because Christ shed His blood, He is the mediator of the new covenant.

1. A mediator is one who "stands between" two parties.
2. Gal. 3:19 - Moses was the mediator of the Old Covenant.
3. Ex. 20:18-19 - Moses stood between God and Israel.
4. 1 Tim. 2:5 - Jesus is now the only mediator between God and man.

by means of death, for the redemption of the transgressions under the first covenant - In this statement, the writer is saying that Christ died for the redemption of the transgressions under the first or Old Covenant. Those who were faithful, and yet transgressed, were redeemed by the blood of Christ.

1. 1 Kings 8:46 - There were none under the Old Covenant who did not sin.
2. Ecc. 7:20 – There is not a man on the earth who does not sin.

3. Heb. 10:4 - The blood of animals could not take away sin.
4. Heb. 9:15 - Christ died to redeem those who were faithful such as Moses, David, Elijah, and numerous others in the Old Testament.

   Illustration of Forgiveness in the Old Testament: The faithful under the Old Testament were forgiven of their sins on credit until the blood of Christ could be shed to pay the price in actual fact. It is much like giving a man a check for some merchandise on Saturday, knowing that you have a direct deposit going into the bank on Monday. The man has his money and you have your merchandise and the money is already set up to be deposited. This is the way it was in the Old Testament. The faithful were forgiven on credit so to speak, because God knew that Christ was already set up for a direct deposit of the blood in the bank.
5. Eph. 1:4; 2 Tim. 1:9; Rev. 13:8; Acts 15:18 - These verses clearly show that God planned and purposed to send Christ to die for man, even before He created the world.
6. Also, if the blood of Christ redeemed those who transgressed the first covenant, then it also went back to redeem those who were faithful who lived before the first covenant was given such as Abel, Noah, Abraham, Sarah, Isaac, Jacob, Joseph, and all of the faithful during that time period. This truth is clearly inferred in the passage we are studying and helps to see how all men from Adam to the end of time are redeemed by the blood of Christ.
7. Heb. 9:22 - Without the shedding of blood there is no remission of sins.
8. Rom. 3:25-26 - These verses show that the death of Christ is how God was just in passing over the sins committed in the Old Testament.

that those who are called may receive the promise of the eternal inheritance - The "called" refers to those in both testaments and the eternal inheritance refers to heaven. The meaning is that all the faithful in both testaments can go to heaven because of the blood of Christ.

1. 2 Thess. 2:14 - Men are called today by the gospel.
2. 1 Peter 1:4 - The inheritance we have is in heaven.

Verses 16, 17: *For where there is a testament, there must also of necessity be the death of the testator. For a testament is in force after men are dead, since it has no power at all while the testator lives* – The writer had stated in verse 15 that Christ is the mediator of the new covenant. This means that Christ had to die in order for the New Covenant to go into effect, and that the New Covenant did not go into effect until after His death.

Illustration: This is the same way it is today with a man and his Will. The terms of the "will" does not go into effect until after the man dies.

1. Heb. 10:10 - The New Testament is called a "will."
2. Gal. 4:4 - Christ was born and lived under the Law of Moses.
3. Matt. 23:2, 3 - He taught His disciples to observe and keep the law.
4. Col. 2:14-16 - The Old Law ended when Christ died on the cross.
5. Heb. 10:9 - Christ had to take away the old covenant in order to establish the new, or else God would have had two different covenants in effect at the same time.
6. Heb. 9:16, 17 - This new covenant went into effect after His death.

Verse 18: *Therefore not even the first covenant was dedicated without blood* - There was bloodshed in connection with the giving of the first covenant. It was dedicated with the blood of animals.

1. Ex. 24:5-6 - This records the blood being shed to dedicate the old covenant.
2. Matt. 26:28 - The blood of Jesus dedicated the new covenant.

Verse 19: *For when Moses had spoken every precept to all the people according to the law, he took the blood of calves and goats, with water, scarlet wool, and hyssop, and sprinkled both the book itself and all the people* - Moses took the blood of the animals that had been shed to dedicate the Old Covenant, and, mixing it with water, he sprinkled it on the book and on the people. He likely only sprinkled those people who were closest to him which would represent all the people.

1. Ex. 24:7 - The "book" refers to the "book of the covenant."
2. Ex. 24:8 - This records Moses sprinkling the blood on the people.
3. From Hebrews we learn that there was water mixed with the blood and also that Moses sprinkled the book.
4. A "hyssop" is a plant.
5. Ex. 24:7 - Moses read the book to the people and they agreed to do what it said.

Verse 20: *saying, This is the blood of the covenant which God has commanded you* - Thus the Old Testament had been dedicated by the blood of animals. It sealed the agreement that God had made with Israel. After sprinkling the blood on the book and people, Moses said, "Behold the blood of the covenant which the Lord has made with you concerning all these words" (Ex. 24:8).

Verse 21: *Then likewise he sprinkled with blood both the tabernacle and all the vessels of the ministry* - The sprinkling of the tabernacle did not occur at the same time as the sprinkling of the book and the people. This occurred much later after the tabernacle had been built.

1. Ex. 40:9-11 - This may be the sprinkling of the tabernacle with blood. It is true that Moses mentions "anointing oil," but in addition was likely the sprinkling of blood and water.
2. Lev. 8:24 – Blood was sprinkled on altar when making atonement for sin.

Verse 22: *And according to the law almost all things are purified with blood, and without shedding of blood there is no remission* - The law of Moses required that everything defiled be purified or cleansed by blood. Every sin under the old law required atonement and no atonement could be made without blood.

1. Lev. 17:11 - It was the blood that made atonement for the soul.
2. Matt. 26:28 - This explains why Christ had to shed His blood for the remission of sins.

SPECIAL NOTE: Beginning in verse 23, the writer begins showing that the sacrifices of the New Testament are superior to those of the Old. He will continue his discussion of the *superior sacrifice of Jesus* through chapter 10:18. Actually, this is a continuation of the superiority of the New Covenant over the Old Covenant which he began in chapter 8:6, because this shows that the *sacrifices of the New Covenant are superior to those offered under the Old.*

Verse 23: *Therefore it was necessary that the copies of the things in the heavens should be purified with these* - Since almost all things were by the law purged with blood, it was necessary for these patterns that pictured things to come to be purified or cleansed by the blood of animals.

1. Heb. 10:1 - The law contained shadows of good things to come.
2. Col. 2:16-17 – Some of the regulations were also a shadow of things to come.

but the heavenly things themselves with better sacrifices than these - The heavenly things refer to the things in the New Covenant. Since the heavenly things were superior to the Old Testament shadows, it was necessary therefore that better sacrifices be offered to purify the heavenly things.

1. Eph. 1:3 - Under the New Covenant Christians are in heavenly places when they are in Christ.
2. By using the terms "heavenly things" and "heavenly places" to describe the blessings of the New Covenant, it seems that the Holy Spirit is seeking to emphasize the higher degree of spiritual blessings of the new arrangement as opposed to some of the "earthly" and "temporal" blessings of Judaism.

Verse 24: *For Christ has not entered the holy places made with hands, which are copies of the true* - This further explains the reason for the better sacrifices of the New Covenant. Christ has not entered into holy places made with hands - like the Old Testament tabernacle which was only a type or shadow of things to come in the New Covenant.

1. Col. 2:16-17 - The law contained shadows or figures of things to come.
2. Heb. 9:9 - The tabernacle was a figure for the time then present.

but into heaven itself, now to appear in the presence of God for us - This explains where our High Priest is and also what He is doing. He is in heaven itself - in the very presence of God - and He is there to intercede „for us."

1. Heb. 4:14-16 - We have a great High Priest who is passed into the heavens and He is there to help us.
2. 1 John 2:1 - He is our advocate with the Father. He pleads our case and takes up for us.
3. Heb. 7:25 - He will always be there to help us. He is always praying for us.

4. Remember that the Judaizers could say, "We have a high priest who is dressed in the garments of the high priest and who is personally right here in Jerusalem. But where is your high priest as a Christian?" The Christian, after reading the Book of Hebrews, could answer, "He is in the true Most Holy Place of which Most Holy Place was only a type. He is in heaven itself in the very presence of God Himself and He is there for us!"

Verse 25: *not that He should offer Himself often, as the high priest enters the Most Holy Place every year with blood of another* - Christ did not have to offer Himself again and again like the Old Testament High Priest who went into the Most Holy Place every year to offer the blood of animals for sin.

1. Lev. 16 - This chapter tells about the High Priest entering the Most Holy Place every year with the blood of animals.
2. Christ only made one sacrifice for sin which will be expounded on later.

Verse 26: *He then would have had to suffer often since the foundation of the world* - If Christ had had to offer Himself every year, like the Old Testament High Priest had to offer the blood of animals, then He would have had to suffer again and again from the very beginning. But such was not the case as Paul states in the next part of the verse.

but now, once at the end of the ages, He has appeared to put away sin by the sacrifice of Himself - Instead of having to suffer often, He appeared once for all time to put away sin by the sacrifice of Himself. There is no need for Him to suffer again and again because He has "put away" sin by His sacrifice. Continual sacrifice is not needed when a sacrifice can obtain absolute forgiveness. Thus, Jesus came at the end of the ages and put away sin by His sacrifice on Calvary.

1. The Jewish age lasted about 1500 years, and it was at the end of these years that He appeared to give His life for sin. The Jewish state, as it was in the OT would only last about forty years after Jesus died for sin. Then the Romans would come and destroy the temple completely and forever.

2. Matt. 24:3, 6, 14 - There was an end to come during the generation that lived when Jesus was on earth (Matt. 24:34). This could not be referring to the end of the material world because such did not occur. Therefore, as the context of Matthew 24:1-34 clearly shows, Jesus was referring to the end of the Jewish state with the total destruction of the temple.

3. 1 Peter 4:7 - There was an end at hand in Peter's day.

4. I personally believe that all the above references refer to the end of Judaism and the Jewish "age" which occurred in 70 A.D.——which is also a type of the end of the world as we will know it.

5. Heb. 10:4 - Animal sacrifices could not put away sin, but the sacrifices of Christ did.

Verse 27: *And as it is appointed for men to die once, but after this the judgment* - Just as men die once and then face the judgment, so Christ only had to die for sins once.

1. It is important to realize that here the Hebrew writer is simply stating a general rule concerning death to which there have been and will be exceptions. For example, some of them are:
   a. Gen. 5:24; Heb. 11:5 - Enoch did not die.
   b. 2 Kings 2:11 - Elijah did not die.
   c. John 11:1-44 - Lazarus, no doubt, died twice.
   d. Matt. 9:18-26 - Jairus' daughter, no doubt, died twice.
   e. 1 Cor. 15:51-52; 1 Thess. 4:17 - Those who are alive when the Lord returns will not die.

2. 2 Cor. 5:10; Matt. 25:31-46 - These verses, along with the one we are studying, clearly show that there is only

going to be one general judgment. Paul does not state
how long after death the judgment will be, he simply
states that it is as sure as death.
3. Heb. 9:28 - The statement about Christ is according to
the rule with no exceptions being considered.

Verse 28: *so Christ was offered once to bear the sins of many*
- Just as men only die once, so Christ only died once for the
sins of man.

1. Matt. 20:28 - Christ gave His life a ransom for many.
2. The word "once" means once for all time. It is the same
word used in Jude 1:3 to show that "the faith" was once
for all time delivered to the saints.
3. Isa. 53:6 - God laid on Jesus the iniquity of us all.

To those who eagerly wait for Him He will appear a second
time, apart from sin, for salvation - Those who "look" for Him
are Christians and it is to them that He will appear the second time with eternal salvation in the new heaven and new
earth. His second coming will be "without sin" because He
is not coming the second time to give Himself for sin. He will
come without giving Himself for sin. He will come with eternal and complete salvation to those who look for Him.

1. John 14:1-3 - He promised to come again—not again
and again.
2. Acts 1:10-11 - The two angels said He would come in
like manner as He ascended which is personally and
visibly.
3. Matt. 24:36-25:13 - Christians are to be always looking for and ready for His coming.
4. 2 Tim. 4:8 - Christians will love His appearing.
5. Matt. 10:30 - While it is true that we are saved from
our past and present sins now, it is also true that we
will be saved eternally in heaven at the Second Coming
of Christ.
6. 2 Pet. 1:10-11 – While we are saved from the penalty

and guilt of sin in the kingdom here, there is also an "entrance" that will be supplied to us into the ultimate state of the kingdom at His coming. In that state of the kingdom we will experience salvation from the very presence of sin.

7. 1 Pet. 1:9 – There is salvation in heaven that comes at the "end of your faith." This will occur when Jesus returns the second time.

HEBREWS
Chapter Ten

JESUS OFFERED A SUPERIOR SACRIFICE

SPECIAL NOTE: In the first eighteen verses of this chapter, the writer continues his discussion of the superior sacrifice of the New Covenant. We are blessed in Hebrews 10 to have revealed to us the reality of the "better" and *superior sacrifice of Jesus* and the manifold blessings we receive as we trust in Him.

Verse 1: *For the law, having a shadow of the good things to come, and not the very image of the things* - The Law of Moses contained shadows or types of things that were to come in the New Covenant. They represented or prefigured things to come but were not the things themselves.

1. Col. 2:16, 17 - The Law of Moses contained shadows of things to come.
    Illustration: House plans are a shadow of a house but not the house itself. They give an idea of what the house will look like but not really what it actually be.
2. Aaron, Moses, Joshua, David, etc. were all types of Christ.
3. All of the sacrifices under the law were a type of the sacrifice of Christ.
4. The tabernacle was a type of both the church and heaven.

can never with these same sacrifices, which they offer continually year by year, make those who approach perfect - The sacrifices offered under the old system did not provide absolute forgiveness for those under that system.

Verse 2: *for then would they not have ceased to be offered? For the worshipers, once purified, would have had no more consciousness of sins* - Repeated sacrifices would not have been necessary if absolute forgiveness had been obtained. A paid debt does not need repeated payments. The repeated sacrifices offered under the old system made them conscious of sins, but did not free them from it. This helps to show that there was a deficiency in the old covenant. The very fact that the sacrifices of the Old Covenant were offered year by year continually proves that the sins were still there and had not been taken away. Illustration: Medicine that cures does not have to be continually taken, and if it does it shows that the disease is still there.

Verse 3: *But in those sacrifices there is a reminder of sins every year* - In those sacrifices offered there was a reminder that sins remained and that there was no absolute remission.

1. They were reminded that the sins existed and the continued offering of sacrifices proved that they had not been actually removed.
2. Cor. 11:23-25 - Observe the contrast: they had to remember their sins, but we remember Christ. What a difference!!!

Verse 4: *For it is not possible that the blood of bulls and goats could take away sins* - This verse clearly answers the question, "Were the sacrifices of the Old Testament able to cleanse one from sin?" Answer: It was not possible.

Verse 5: *Therefore when He came into the world, He said Sacrifice and offering You did not desire, But a body You have prepared for Me* – This was a quote from Psalm 40:6-8. God was not satisfied with the blood of animals as a sacrifice for sin. They could not meet the demands of justice. However, if Christ came to the earth, lived sinless, and then died for sin, the demands of justice would be met. Hence, there was a body prepared for Him to live in.

The statement "when He came into the world" affirms the pre-earthly existence of the "Word." (Jn. 1:1-3).

1. Animals, angels, nor mere men could pay the price for sin. Only the sinless Son of God could atone for the sins of the whole world. No angel could His place have taken, Highest of High though He. The one on the cross forsaken was one of the God-Head Three.
2. John 17:5 - He was with the Father before He came to the earth.
3. Heb. 2:14-17 - He was made partaker of "flesh and blood."
4. John 1:14 - He was "made flesh."
5. Lk. 1:30-35 - He was born of a virgin.

Verse 6: *In burnt offerings and sacrifices for sin You had no pleasure* - They could not take away sin and, thus, God was not pleased or satisfied with them as an offering for sin.

Verse 7: *Then I said, Behold, I have come—in the volume of the book it is written of Me—to do Your will, O God* - Since God was not pleased with those sacrifices, Christ came to offer a sacrifice that would please Him. This was according to God's will. The "volume of the book" probably refers to the Old Testament, especially the first five books. Those books predicted, both directly and indirectly, that Christ would die as the sacrifice for sin.

1. Gen. 3:15 - The statement to the devil that He would bruise the seed of the woman is generally considered a prophecy concerning the sacrifice of Christ.
2. Gen. 22:18; 49:10; Deut. 18:15-18 - These passages all predict that Christ was coming into the world to do God's will and bless all nations by doing it.
3. Ex. 12 - The Passover lamb was a type of the sacrifice of Christ.
4. 1 Corinthians 5:7 - Christ is our Passover. Just as the

blood of the Passover lamb caused God to pass over the houses where the blood was applied, in the same way the blood of Christ causes God to pass over the sins of those who trust in Him.
5. John 6:38 - Jesus came down from heaven to do the will of the Father.

Verse 8: *Previously saying, Sacrifice and offering, burnt offerings, and offerings for sin You did not desire, nor had pleasure in them (which are offered according to the law)* - This is simply a restatement of facts he had already revealed concerning the inability of animal sacrifices to take away sin or meet the demands of God's justice. However, in this verse, the writer adds that they were offered "according to the law." He is here stressing the fact that the old law demanded the offering of animal sacrifices.

Verse 9: *then He said, "Behold, I have come to do Your will, O God." He takes away the first that He may establish the second* - In verse 8, he has shown that God was not pleased with the animal sacrifices of the Old Testament, and yet they were offered by the authority of the Law of Moses. He now points out that Christ came to do God's will which was to offer a sacrifice that would please Him. But in order to do that, He had to take away the old law that demanded animal sacrifices, so that He could establish the new law that would allow Him to be the sacrifice for sin.

1. Heb. 8:7 - The "first" refers to the first covenant which was the Law of Moses. (See also Heb. 8:13).
2. Heb. 8:7 - The "second" refers to the second or new covenant of Christ. (See also Heb. 8:8-13)
3. The verse simply means that Christ took away the first or old covenant that demanded animal sacrifices for sin in order that He might establish the second or new covenant which would allow Him to be the sacrifice for sin.
4. Heb. 7:18-19 - The old law was set aside or abolished.

5. Heb. 7:12 - The law, sacrifices, and priesthood of the Old Covenant stood or fell together.

Verse 10: *by that will we have been sanctified through the offering of the body of Jesus Christ once for all* – It is by Christ doing God's will that believers are justified. This verse explains how we are sanctified or set apart and made holy. It is "through the offering of the body of Christ once for all." A body was prepared for Christ (10:5), but in order to offer Himself as a sacrifice for sin, the old law that demanded animal sacrifices had to be taken away (10:9). This is exactly what happened. We are now made holy by the offering of the body of Christ once for all. This makes it possible for us to be sanctified through the "will" of Christ.

1. Heb. 10:10 - We are sanctified through the offering of the body of Jesus Christ.
2. 1 Pet. 2:24 - He bore our sins in His own body on the tree.
3. Jn. 17:17 - We are sanctified through the truth.
4. 1 Cor. 6:11 - We are sanctified by the Holy Spirit.
5. 1 Cor. 1:2 - We are sanctified "in Christ."
6. Gal. 3:26-27 - The Spirit teaches us to be baptized into Christ and thereby we are set apart and made holy. All of this is possible through our faith in the offering of the body of Jesus Christ.

SPECIAL NOTE: Jesus had to take away the first (or old) law in order to establish the second (or new) law, or else God would have had two laws in effect at the same time. One law would have said to offer animal sacrifices (Heb. 10:8). The other would have said we are sanctified through the sacrifice of Jesus Christ (Heb. 10:10). One law would have said the priests must be of the tribe of Levi and family of Aaron (Ex. 28:1). The other would have said all the people of God are priests (1 Peter 2:5, 9). Thus, it is perfectly clear that Jesus had to take away the Old Covenant in order to establish the New.

Verse 11: *And every priest stands ministering daily and offering repeatedly the same sacrifices, which can never take away sins* - The priests offered daily sacrifices in the morning and evening, in addition to various other sacrifices. They offered the same sacrifices over and over which could never atone for sins. They offered many sacrifices which were powerless to take away sins and this is mentioned to contrast their many sacrifices with the one sacrifice of Christ.

1. Ex. 29:38-46 - This is the law regarding the daily sacrifices.
2. Numbers 28:3-4 – These verses also deal with those offerings.

Verse 12: *But this Man, after He had offered one sacrifice for sins forever, sat down at the right hand of God* - In verse 11, the writer had stated that the priests under the old law offered sacrifices repeatedly and even daily. But Christ offered one sacrifice and He offered that one sacrifice forever, never to be repeated.

1. Heb. 2:14-17 - He had already shown that Jesus became a man.
2. Heb. 2:9 – He had already shown that He tasted death for every man.

sat down at the right hand of God - This is the big difference between the sacrifices of the Old Covenant and the one sacrifice of the New. Their priests stand (Heb. 10:11), emphasizing that their work is never really completed. Christ, however, "sat down" after His sacrifice which proves that His one sacrifice was sufficient.

1. The Jews might say, "Just look at our priests, they offer sacrifices every morning and evening. And come see our High Priest as he walks in the temple on the Day of Atonement to offer the animals as a sacrifice for our sins." To this the Christian could reply, "Our High

Priest has made one sacrifice for sins forever and, since it doesn't need repeating, He has sat down."

2. The fact that Christ has "sat down" does not mean that He's not doing anything. He upholds all things (Heb. 1:3) and He makes intercession for us (Heb. 7:25) as well as numerous other things. But as far as the subject under consideration is concerned—which is the sacrifice for sins—He has completed it and sat down.

Verse 13: *from that time waiting till His enemies are made His footstool* - The enemies of Christ are Satan, demons, sin, death, etc. The idea here is that all things are yet to be made subject to Christ, either by cheerful submission to His will, or by being crushed beneath His power. It was the custom of that time for conquerors to put their feet on the necks of their enemies, or walk over them, as a symbol of their subjection and defeat. This is what Christ will one day do to His enemies – He will totally defeat them.

1. Ps. 110:1 - This was prophesied of Christ. In Acts 2:34-35 Peter quoted the prophecy in the first gospel sermon and applied it to Christ.
2. Heb. 1:13 – The writer had already used this statement in this letter.
3. 1 Cor. 15:25-26 — The last enemy that Christ will destroy on this earth is death.
4. Rev. 20:10 – Satan will also be destroyed.

Verse 14: *For by one offering He has perfected forever those who are being sanctified* - By one sacrifice He has obtained absolute forgiveness for those who are sanctified in Christ. "Perfected" does not refer to being "perfect" as far as holy living is concerned, but "perfect" as far as absolute forgiveness is concerned. The word must be understood according to the context and here he is discussing sacrifices for sins.

1. Heb. 7:11 - There was no perfection under the Levitical system.

2. Heb. 7:19 - The law made nothing perfect, but the bringing in of a better hope did.
3. Col. 1:27 – We are made perfect in Christ.

Verse 15: *But the Holy Spirit also witnesses to us; for after He had said before* - In this verse, the writer points out that the Holy Spirit is also a witness that our sins are absolutely and totally forgiven under the New Covenant in Christ. The Holy Spirit had said, in their own Hebrew writings, that under the New Covenant sins would be absolutely forgiven.

1. Jer. 31:33-34 - Notice that what Jeremiah said is attributed to the Holy Spirit.
2. 2 Peter 1:20-21 - The prophets spoke as they were moved by the Holy Spirit.

Verses 16, 17: *This is the covenant that I will make with them after those days, says the LORD: I will put My laws into their hearts, and in their minds I will write them, then He adds, Their sins and their lawless deeds I will remember no more* - In this section, the Hebrew writer again quotes the prophecy of Jeremiah that he had used earlier in chapter 8:10-12. He quoted the prophecy in chapter 8 to show that the Old Covenant had foretold the taking away of the Old Covenant and the establishing of the New. He now quotes the same prophecy, but not for the same reason. Here he quotes it to emphasize that under the new covenant, "sins and iniquities would be remembered no more." And this proves that, according to the Holy Spirit sins would be absolutely forgiven in the new arrangement. The Jews might not accept what he had said so far about absolute forgiveness, but when he called their own Scriptures as a witness, that should settle it for them.

1. Heb. 10:3 - Under the Old Covenant, there was a "remembrance again made of sins," but under the new they are "remembered no more."
2. Heb. 8:10-12 - Observe how he used the words "heart" and "mind" interchangeably in the two quotations

proving that the heart referred to in the Bible is the mind or knowing part of man and not the physical heart.

3. Rom. 8:16 - The Holy Spirit was a witness through the words of the prophet Jeremiah concerning the things Paul was discussing. In the same way, the Holy Spirit witnesses with us through the words of the apostles and prophets of the New Testament.

Verse 18: *Now where there is remission of these, there is no longer an offering for sin* - If a sacrifice provides absolute forgiveness of sins, then there is no need for any other sacrifice. If the Jews asked, "Where are your sacrifices to offer for sins?" The Christian could answer, "The sacrifice that provides absolute forgiveness has been offered once for all time. Therefore, we need no other."

SPECIAL NOTE: This ends the section of the book dealing with the superior sacrifice of Christ. The remainder deals with exhorting and encouraging them in light of the truths that have been presented.

Verse 19: *Therefore, brethren, having boldness to enter the Holiest by the blood of Jesus* - The "holiest" here must refer to heaven which is the anti-type of the Most Holy Place under the Old Covenant. Because we have absolute forgiveness, we have confidence and assurance of heaven by the blood of Jesus. Boldness means fearlessness in the face of danger as well as assurance and confidence.

Verse 20: *by a new and living way which He consecrated for us* - We have assurance of entering into heaven by a new manner or method which is Christ and His sacrifice. It is not only a new way, but also a living way in contrast with the dead animals of the old system.

1. John 14:6 - Jesus is the way to the Father.
2. Isa. 35:8 - This "way of holiness" was prophesied

by Isaiah.

3. **Acts 9:2, 9, 23 - Christianity is called "the way."**
4. **Consecrated means dedicated.**

through the veil, that is, His flesh - Just as the High Priest went into the Most Holy Place through the large curtain that separated the Holy Place from the Most Holy Place, so we get to heaven through the death of Christ.

1. The idea is that both by the veil of the temple and the body of Jesus there is a way of access to God. He did not say nor mean there was a resemblance between the veil and Christ in every way.
2. When the High Priest went from the Holy Place into the Most Holy Place, he had to go through the veil to get there, but our way to heaven is through the slain body (flesh) of Jesus.

Verse 21: *and having a High Priest over the house of God* - He had already discussed the fact that Jesus is our High Priest.

1. Heb. 3:1; 4:14; 7:26 - Jesus is our great High Priest.
2. 1 Tim. 3:15 - The house of God is the church.

Verse 22: *let us draw near with a true heart in full assurance of faith* - Since we have such a High Priest, we should draw near to God with a pure and sincere heart and with full confidence in our High Priest.

having our hearts sprinkled from an evil conscience - The word "sprinkled" must be a symbol for cleansed. We are to have our hearts cleansed from an evil conscience.

1. 1 John 1:7 - We are cleansed by the blood of Jesus.
2. 1 Peter 1:2 - Peter refers to the sprinkling of the blood of Jesus.
3. Heb. 12:24 - Later the writer of Hebrews will refer to the blood of sprinkling.

4. Lev. 16:14-15 - The background for referring to our cleansing as the "sprinkling of the blood of Jesus" has its foundation in the Old Testament. Just as the high priest sprinkled the blood of animals on the mercy seat in the Most Holy Place and thus cleansed the people in a sense, so the sprinkling of the blood of Jesus cleanses us.
5. Heb. 9:14 - It is the blood of Jesus that purges our conscience.

our bodies washed with pure water - This can only refer to baptism since that is the only way "water" is connected with our salvation. The fact that our "bodies" are washed seems to show that baptism is an immersion.

1. 1 Peter 3:21 - Peter connects the water of baptism with our having a good conscience.
2. Eph. 5:26; Acts 22:16 - These verses also show that there is a "washing of water" that is connected with our salvation.

Verse 23: *Let us hold fast the confession of our hope without wavering* - These Hebrew Christians were suffering persecution and were being tempted to go back to Judaism. Thus, they needed encouragement to help them overcome doubting and discouragement. They had professed faith in Christ and the gospel, and the writer says, "Hold fast that profession."

1. Heb. 3:13 - They were in danger of departing from God.
2. Heb. 12:4 - They were suffering persecution.
3. Heb. 4:14 - They had already been encouraged to hold fast their profession.
4. Rev. 2:25; 3:3, 11 - Churches need to "hold fast."

for He who promised is faithful - This was the main reason they needed to hold fast. God is faithful to do what He has promised. This is a truth that all Christians need to keep in mind at all times.

1. 1 Cor. 10:13 — God is faithful not to allow us to be tempted above what we are able to bear.
2. 1 John 1:9 - He is faithful to forgive us our sins.
3. Rev. 1:5-6 - Jesus is called the faithful witness.

Verse 24: *And let us consider one another in order to stir up love and good works* - They needed to encourage one another by stirring each other up to love and good works.

1. Notice that the verse does not say that we are to "provoke one another," but rather we are to provoke one another to certain actions—love and good works. The only provoking that some brethren do is stirring up anger.
2. Provoke means to excite to some action or feeling.

Verse 25: *not forsaking the assembling of ourselves together* - Christians are commanded to assemble together for edification and to worship God. However, because of the persecution and temptation brought on by the Jews, some had already stopped or quit assembling with the saints for worship and encouragement.

1. Forsake means to give up, renounce, to leave, abandon.
2. Acts 20:7 – Christians at Troas came together on the first day of the week.
3. 1 Cor. 11:20 - The Corinthians met together.
4. 1 Cor. 11:33 - They came together to eat the Lord's Supper.
5. 1 Cor. 14:23 - They came together for instructions and teaching.
6. It is not necessarily wrong to miss an assembly for worship but it is wrong to intentionally forsake it altogether.

7. Forsaking the assembly was a sign that they had forsaken Christ.

as is the manner of some, but exhorting one another - Instead of forsaking the assembly, they needed to exhort one another and so much the more as they saw the day approaching. From this statement and what follows, it is obvious that some had already abandoned Christ and this was clear because they had stopped meeting with the saints.

SPECIAL STUDY: THE DAY APPROACHING - What is the day they could see approaching? There are at least three different opinions as to what "day" is referred to. They are as follows:

1. The "Second Coming of Christ."

    a. 2 Peter 3:10; 1 Thess. 5:2 - It is called the day of the Lord. (See also 2 Peter 2:9; Jude 1:6).
    b. However, the day under consideration in Hebrews 10:24 is a day that they could see approaching.
    c. Matt. 24:36 - Since no one knows the "day" when Christ will return, I don't see how this could be the day they could see approaching.

2. The "Destruction of Jerusalem" in 70 A.D.

    a. Mal. 4:5 - It is called the "day" of the Lord.
    b. The destruction of Jerusalem is discussed in the Book of Hebrews and likely even in this chapter.
    c. Heb. 8:13 - This statement likely refers to the destruction of Jerusalem.
    d. Heb. 10:37 - This shows that the destruction of the temple was near.
    e. Heb. 12:27 - This may also have a primary reference to the destruction of Jerusalem even though the ultimate reference likely refers to the end of the world.

f. The majority of commentators I have read think that this is the day referred to and this could very well be the day. It will fit the context of the Book of Hebrews and they could possibly see the signs that that day was approaching even though I am not convinced that this was the case.

3. The "First Day of the Week."

a. It seems to me that the "day approaching"' most likely refers to the first day of the week. Though I would never insist that one must believe this, it seems to me to be more natural for it to refer to the "day" when the saints assemble. This is what he is discussing in this verse and it seems consistent to me that this is the day that the writer is referring to.

b. Rev. 1:10 - The first day of the week is called the "Lord's Day."

c. Mk. 16:9 - It was the day that Jesus arose.

d. Acts 2:1 - It is the day on which the church was established.

e. Acts 20:7; 1 Cor. 16:1-2 - It is the day when the Christians assembled.

f. This was surely a day that they could see approaching, even more so than they could see the day when Jerusalem was destroyed.

g. Some object to this view by saying that, if this is the case, one would have to start exhorting on Monday and increase "the more" as Sunday approached. In other words, there would have to be daily exhorting. And in their situation with the persecutions and temptations they faced on a daily basis, I think this is precisely the case. They were instructed to "exhort one another daily" (Heb. 3:13).

h. Some may say that we don't exhort one another like Hebrews 10:25 says, but neither do we exhort one another daily like Hebrews 3:13 admonishes. But hopefully we would if necessary.

Special Note: For more on this subject see Appendix # 2 concerning "Forsaking the Assembly."

Verse 26: *For if we sin willfully after we have received the knowledge of the truth* - The reference here is to those who forsake (leave off, abandon) assembling with the saints. The reference is to continual habitual practice of sin as a way of life in rebellion against God. It does not refer to isolated acts of sin or even sinning on purpose which we all do, but it refers to the continual habitual practice of deliberate sin which in this case is forsaking the assembly which proves that they had abandoned Christ.

1. 1 John 3:9 - "Sin" here, as the context clearly shows, refers to the continual practice of sin as a way of life—a mind that is set on sin like Satan.
2. Rom. 3:23 – All sin and fall short of what God expects including faithful Christians.
3. 1 Jn. 1:8 – If we say we have no sin we deceive ourselves.
4. 1 Jn. 1:9 – If we acknowledge (admit) our sin He is faithful to forgive us.
5. 1 Jn. 1:7 – Part of walking in the light is admitting that we need the blood of Jesus to continually cleanse us from sins that we constantly commit.

there no longer remains a sacrifice for sins - There will never be another sacrifice offered for sins. If these Jewish believers rejected the sacrifice of Christ by sinning willfully and rejecting Him, then they rejected the only sacrifice that can take away sin. There is no other.

1. Heb. 10:12 - Jesus made "one sacrifice for sins forever"

and there will never be another.
2. Heb. 10:18 – The writer had just stated, "there is no more offering for sin."

Verse 27: *but a certain fearful expectation of judgment* - This is what those who continually sin willfully by rejecting Jesus and His sacrifice have to look forward to - judgment and fiery indignation.

1. Heb. 9:27 - He had already referred to the judgment.
2. Heb. 6:2 - He had already stated it is an eternal judgment.

and fiery indignation which will devour the adversaries - The "fiery indignation" refers to hell which will devour eat up or consume those who oppose or resist Christ.

1. Devour means to eat up hungrily; to consume or destroy with devastating force; to swallow up.
2. Adversary means one who opposes, contends with, or resists; opponent; enemy.
3. Matt. 12:30 - All those who are not with Christ are His adversaries.
4. Fire is a symbol of God's judgment on the wicked.
   a. Gen. 19:24 - Sodom was destroyed by fire.
   b. Lev. 10:1, 2 - Fire destroyed Nadab and Abihu.
   c. Num. 16:35 - Fire consumed the men involved in the rebellion of Korah.
   d. Matt. 3:11-12 - John announced that some would be baptized with fire.
   e. Mk. 9:43; 44-48 - The fire of hell will not be put out.
   f. 2 Thess. 1:7-9 - Christ will be revealed from heaven in flaming fire.
   g. Heb. 12:29 - God is a consuming fire to His enemies.

Verse 28: *Anyone who has rejected Moses' law dies without mercy on the testimony of two or three witnesses* - Those who had no regard for the Law of Moses died on the testimony of two or three witnesses for sins of rebellion. This was the general rule to which there were, no doubt, exceptions.

1. Heb. 10:26-28 - This helps to understand that "sinning willfully" was the same as those who "rejected" Moses law. It was therefore not sins of weakness, ignorance or misunderstanding but sins that involved rebellion and rejection.
2. Deut. 17:2-7 - This is an example of one being stoned on the testimony of two or three witnesses.

Verse 29: *Of how much worse punishment, do you suppose, will he be thought worthy who has trampled the Son of God underfoot, counted the blood of the covenant by which he was sanctified a common thing, and insulted the Spirit of grace?* - Here Paul asks of how much more severe punishment would one be worthy who: (1) Treads underfoot the Son of God; (2) counts the blood of Christ an unholy or common thing; and (3) insulted the Holy Spirit. The answer is obvious: The one who does such things deserves far more severe punishment than death by stoning. And it is also implied that those who do such will receive it.

1. This verse shows the seriousness of sinning willfully which in this context is forsaking or abandoning the assembly.
2. The words "worse punishment" proves that the punishment in hell is far worse than death by stoning.
    a. Matt. 25:46 - It is eternal punishment.
    b. Rom. 2:8-9 - It is tribulation and anguish.
    c. Heb. 10:27 - It is fiery indignation.
3. Lk. 12:47-48 - This verse indicates that there will be degrees of punishment for the wicked.
4. 2 Peter 2:20-22 - Peter teaches that it is worse for the Christian who goes back into sin than for non-Chris-

tians.

5. The words "was sanctified" prove that a person who at one time was sanctified can be in danger of being lost.

6. There are many passages that teach that a child of God can so sin as to be eternally lost in hell. (Ezek. 18:24-28; John 15:1-6; Matt. 25:14-30; 2 Pet. 1:10; 1 Cor. 10:12; Gal. 5:4; Rev. 3:5).

Verse 30: *For we know Him who said, Vengeance is Mine, I will repay, says the Lord, and again, The LORD will judge His people* – The writer reminds them that they knew that God is a God of truth, justice, power, holiness, and one who carries out His promises. The statement "vengeance is Mine, I will repay" is quoted to remind them that God will certainly, in due time, repay those who oppose and resist Him.

1. Deut. 32:35 – Their foot shall slide in due time but vengeance belongs to God.

2. Deut. 32:36 - "The Lord shall judge His people" is quoted to show that God will not allow even the sins of His own children to pass.

3. Rom. 12:19 - Paul used this same statement here.

Verse 31: *It is a fearful thing to fall into the hands of the living God* - For the person under consideration in these verses, who is one who continually sins willfully as a way of life, it is a fearful thing to fall into the hands of God. Why? Because He is a God of vengeance to those who continually refuse and reject Him. God is a consuming fire to His enemies (Heb. 12:29).

1. Rom. 11:22 - God is both good and severe. Good to those who trust Him, but severe to those who refuse.

2. Psalm 23:4 – It is not a fearful thing for a Christian to die. In fact, he will fear no evil.

SPECIAL NOTE: Beginning with verse 32, he begins encouraging them. After he severely warned them, he encourages, as he did earlier in chapter 6.

1. Heb. 5:11-6:8 - He rebuked them for lack of growth and then warned them against falling away.
2. Heb. 6:9 - He then had words of encouragement for them.
3. 2 Thess. 3:13 - This, as we have already observed, was Paul's manner of softening hard statements.

Verse 32: *But recall the former days in which, after you were illuminated, you endured a great struggle with sufferings* - This verse indicates that they had suffered severe trials and hardship. He encourages them by referring to how they had overcome a great fight of affliction in the past.

1. Acts 8:1; 11:19 - The persecution they experienced in other days possibly refers to the persecution that resulted in the death of Stephen.
2. Acts 12:1-3 - Herod had also persecuted the church of Jerusalem in the past.
3. Heb. 12:4 - This verse does not rule out the death of Stephen or others, but only means that those receiving the letter were evidently not having to die at that particular time, though some may have died in time past.

Verse 33: *partly while you were made a spectacle both by reproaches and tribulations, and partly while you became companions of those who were so treated* - In former days they had been exposed to public shame, abuse, and had been openly afflicted personally. Others, who may not have been personally involved, ministered to those who were mistreated.

1. Heb. 6:10 – They ministered to other saints who were in need.
2. Heb. 5:12 – They had not grown in knowledge as they should but they were faithful.

Verse 34: *for you had compassion on me in my chains, and joyfully accepted the plundering of your goods, knowing that* *you have a better and an enduring possession for yourselves in heaven* - They had compassion on Paul while he was a prisoner at some point in the past. They had experienced loss of their material goods and they had done so joyfully, because they knew that they had in heaven something better and more permanent than their earthly possessions.

1. The phrase "in my chains" in the NKJV is questioned by some, but is upheld by Young`s Literal Translation as well as the Greek-English Interlinear by both Berry and Green.
2. Acts 28:16, 20, 30, 31 - Paul was in chains in Rome and this is one of the reasons that I favor the view that he was the author.
3. Philemon v. 10; Phil. 1:7, 16; Col. 4:18; Eph. 6:20 - Paul often referred to his chains.
4. Heb. 13:24 - The writer of Hebrews was in Italy (Rome) and in chains. This fits Paul even if he did not write the book.
5. Matt. 6:19, 20 - We are to lay up treasures "in heaven."
6. Col. 3:1-2 - We are to set our affections on things "above."
7. 1 Peter 1:4 - We have an inheritance, incorruptible and undefiled, that fades not away reserved in heaven.

Verse 35: *Therefore do not cast away your confidence, which has great reward* - They are encouraged not to cast away their confidence in Christ and the gospel by going back to Judaism. They would be richly rewarded in the end.

1. 1 Cor. 15:58 - Our labor is not in vain in the Lord.
2. Heb. 11:26 - There is nothing wrong with looking for ward to our reward as motivation for doing right.

Verse 36: *For you have need of endurance, so that after you have done the will of God, you may receive the promise* - They needed to patiently endure in spite of discouragement and persecution, because after they had done God's will in this life they would receive the promise of eternal life in heaven.

1. Heb. 12:1 - Christians must run the Christian race with patience.
2. 2 Peter 1:5-7 - Believers must add patience.
3. Rev. 2:10 - If they are faithful unto death, they will receive a crown of life.
4. 1 John 2:25 - The promise that He has promised us is eternal life.

Verse 37: *For yet a little while, and He who is coming will come and will not tarry* - This is another reason for the Christians to hold fast and not return to Judaism. It would be only a little while until God came in judgment on Jerusalem by means of the Roman Armies.

1. James 5:8 - There was a "coming of Christ" that was "at hand" in the first century. In my judgment this could not refer to His second coming, so it must refer to His coming in judgment on Jerusalem.
2. Heb. 8:13 - He that shall come will come and Judaism would vanish away completely as far as sacrifices, temple worship, and priests are concerned.
3. 1 Peter 4:7 – The end of all things Jewish was at hand and would happen in a little while.

Verse 38: *Now the just shall live by faith; But if anyone draws back, My soul has no pleasure in him* - The statement "the just shall live by faith" is a quotation from Habakkuk 2:4. This states an eternal principle of God, and that is, a person who wants "life" must continue to live by faith no matter what. It is a promise that those who continue to trust God will be taken care of by God. The just shall have "life" only by having "faith." However, if any of these Hebrew Christians drawback, which in this context means leave Christ and go back to Judaism through fear of persecution or influence of the Jews, God will not be pleased with them. He will not be pleased with those who fall away.

1. Rom. 1:17; Gal. 3:11 - Paul quoted the statement of
   Habakkuk on at least two other occasions.
2. Heb. 3:12 – They had been warned about having an
   evil heart of unbelief and departing from God.
3. Heb. 6:1-6 – They had been warned against falling
   away.

Verse 39: *But we are not of those who draw back to perdition,
but of those who believe to the saving of the soul* - These are
words of encouragement, as well as a statement of the confidence that the writer had in them. If these Jewish Christians
left the gospel and returned to Judaism, they would not only
suffer utter destruction in the end, but they would also be destroyed "in a little while" when God came in judgment on Jerusalem. Having mentioned that they are those who "believe
to the saving of the soul" the writer will discuss the subject of
"faith" in some detail in chapter eleven.

Section Three:
THE SUPERIOR POSITION
OF THOSE
IN CHRIST
(Chps. 11:1-13:25)

HEBREWS
Chapter Eleven

JESUS PROVIDES SUPERIOR BLESSINGS

SPECIAL NOTE: Having mentioned faith in chapter 10:38-39, the writer now, in chapter 11, goes into a lengthy discussion of what faith is and what men and women have done because of it. It's an understatement to say the Bible speaks often of the necessity and benefits of "faith" in the life of a disciple of Christ and follower of God. Great men and women of God demonstrated great faith and trust in the face of difficult situations of life. Whether David facing Goliath, Daniel in the lion's den, or Abraham with the unenviable task of offering his own son as a sacrifice on an altar, these faithful followers found the help, strength and peace of God when they trusted in Him above all else. He blessed them with forgiveness and numerous other blessings. But in spite of all He did for them, He has provided something "better" for us. The spiritual *blessings we have in Christ are far superior* to any blessings the Old Covenant saints received (Ephesians 1:3ff). There is *better news for the Hebrews.*

Verse 1: *Now faith is the substance of things hoped for, the evidence of things not seen* - This is an inspired definition of faith. "Faith" is being sure of what we hope for and certain of what we do not see.

1. Faith is complete trust, confidence, or reliance.
2. I would say that faith is being sure concerning things hoped for, and having a conviction concerning things not seen.

Verse 2: *For by it the elders obtained a good report* - Having defined faith in verse one, the writer proceeds to demonstrate what faith has accomplished. The "elders" refer to the ancient heroes of faith in the Old Testament. They "obtained a good report" from God and He approved of them because of their faith. The ancient men and women of God so lived that they obtained positive acceptance from Him.

1. Elder can mean a forefather or ancestor.
2. 1 Tim. 5:1 - The word "elder" does not always refer to the leaders in the church. Sometimes it simply means an older person; either past or present.

Verse 3: *Through faith we understand that the worlds were framed by the word of God, so that things which are seen were not made of things which do appear* - The creation of the world is among the things "not seen" and all of our knowledge of it rests on faith that comes from the word of God (Rom. 10:17). It is "through faith" that we understand that God spoke the world into existence. By His word, the world was brought into existence out of nothing.

1. Heb. 1:2 - The worlds were made by Christ. (See also John 1:1-14; Col. 1:16; Eph. 3:9.)
2. Word is not from *Logos* as in John 1:1, but from the word that is used in Matthew 4:4 and means the spoken word.
3. Gen. 1:3 - God said, "Let there be light and there was light."
4. Psalm 33:6-9 - God commanded and it was done.

SPECIAL STUDY: "THE CREATION"

1. The "days" of creation - There are at least four good reasons for believing the days were ordinary days.
   a. Each day had an evening and a morning (Gen. 1).
   b. Exodus 20:8-11 clearly indicate that the days were ordinary days.
   c. NOTE: In Exodus 20:8-10 Moses had been speaking of ordinary days and then mentions the six days of creation in verse 11.

    d. The word "day" normally means an ordinary day unless the context clearly indicates otherwise. Nothing in the context of Genesis 1 indicates otherwise.

    e. Adam lived through the seventh day, yet died at the age of 930 years (Gen. 5:5).

2. The "Gap Theory" - Some think there is a long gap between Genesis 1:1 and Genesis 1:2. They believe the word "was" in Genesis 1:2 should be "became." It is true that the Hebrew word sometimes can be "became," but the context must demand it when that is the case. The context does not seem to demand it in Genesis 1. Furthermore, Exodus 20:8-11 indicates that God created the heavens, earth, seas, and all that is in them in six regular days. It seems to me that the "Gap Theory" is nothing more than an unnecessary compromise. In my judgment, those who believe in Theistic Evolution simply fail to accept the Bible account as it is written.

3. The "age" of the earth - How old is the earth? Some think it is 6,000 years old because of the dates that are in some Bibles. These dates are probably not correct. Bishop Usher, who figured out these dates, was probably wrong on some of them. There are probably gaps in genealogy records in Matthew 1:1-15 and Luke 3:23-38. However, the gaps in the genealogies do not allow for enough time to make the earth millions of years old. In fact, 6,000 -10,000 years is probably not far off from the actual age of the earth.

4. Jesus and the creation. Jesus said we could read how God made them male and female in the beginning and the place to "read" about it is Genesis chapters 1 & 2. (Matt. 19:4-6; Mk. 10:6-8).

Verse 4: *By faith Abel offered to God a more excellent sacrifice than Cain, through which he obtained witness that he was righteous, God testifying of his gifts; and through it he being dead still speaks* - Some see significance in the fact that Adam and Eve were passed over. They were not regarded as heroes of the faith. The first example that the writer gives is that of Abel. Abel offered the sacrifice that God said to offer, while Cain refused to offer what God commanded or else he offered it with the wrong attitude or perhaps both reasons. We don't know exactly how God testified of His gift, but now God testifies that Abel's gift rendered him righteous through His word in the book of Hebrews. Abel's influence lives on. His example still says trust, work and worship God as He deserves and demands.

1. Gen. 4:1-5 - These verses give the account of the offerings of Cain and Abel.
2. That God told them what to offer is obvious from the following:
   a. Heb. 11:4 - Abel offered by faith,
   b. Rom. 10:17 - Faith comes from hearing the word of God.
   c. Rom. 2:11 - If God told Abel, He also told Cain.
3. 1 John 3:12 - This verse tells us exactly why Cain killed Abel.

Verse 5: *By faith Enoch was taken away so that he did not see death, and was not found, because God had taken him; for before he was taken he had this testimony, that he pleased God* - In Genesis 5:22-24, we see that Enoch pleased God by walking with Him. Jude 1:14 says Enoch also prophesied about the coming of the Lord. Where Jude got his information we are not told, but we do know he received it from inspiration.

1. Hebrews 11:5 is a commentary on Genesis 5:24.
2. 1 Kings 2:11 - Elijah and Enoch evidently went to heaven or paradise which is where all saints go at death (Phil. 1:21-23).

Verse 6: *But without faith it is impossible to please Him, for he who comes to God must believe that He is, and that He is a rewarder of those who diligently seek Him* - This proves that man must believe before he responds and that God rewards those who diligently seek Him.

1. Psalm 19:1 - The heavens declare the glory and thus the existence of God.
2. Rom. 1:20 - The power and wisdom of God is seen in things created. There is no excuse for not believing in a Divine Creator.
3. We can see that there is power and design in the establishment of the world. Illustration: If we go on an island and see a house, we would immediately know, because of the design, that a person with intelligence has been there. We would not believe for a minute that a storm came through and built the house.
4. Heb. 3:4 - Every house is built by some man, but He that created all things is God.

Verse 7: *By faith Noah, being divinely warned of things not yet seen, moved with godly fear, prepared an ark for the saving of his household, by which he condemned the world and became heir of the righteousness which is according to faith* - Noah's faith caused him to be sure of things "not yet seen." He believed so strongly that he spent one hundred and twenty years or so building an ark. Faith makes the unseen real.

1. Gen. 6-9 - These chapters give the account of the flood.
2. Gen. 6:12, 13 - Some say a cubit was eighteen inches. Others say about twenty-two inches.
   a. Allowing eighteen inches for a cubit, the ark was 450 feet long, 75 feet wide, and 45 feet high with three stories.
   b. It was very large with as much shipping space as a freight train with over 500 boxcars.
   c. The animals did not have to be full-grown when taken into the ark. Dinosaurs and elephants could

have been very young and small.

3. Gen. 7:11-12 – The water came from two sources. Water gushed up from the ground as well as the rain from above.

4. Gen. 2:5-6 – These verses may indicate that it might not have ever rained before the flood according to some, but we don't really know.

5. Gen. 7:2 - He was to take seven pairs of clean animals and one pair of unclean.

    a. There were fourteen clean animals and two each of the unclean.

    b. Here we see a distinction between clean and unclean animals long before the Law of Moses was given.

6. Gen. 8:20 - As soon as he came out of the ark Noah offered clean animals as a sacrifice which was one reason for taking them in by sevens.

    a. The clean and unclean must refer to those that were to be used for sacrifices and those that were not.

    b. Gen. 9:3 - This verse indicates that Noah could eat all of the animals both clean and unclean. So clean and unclean probably did not refer to eating, but to ones that were used as sacrifices and those that were not used.

7. Gen. 11:7 – This verse is evidence for a universal flood!

    a. If local, why build an ark?

    b. Why build it so big?

    c. Why take birds into the ark if it was just a local one? (Genesis 7:3)

    d. How could a local flood be kept in the same area for over one year without a miracle? Noah entered the ark for seven days and then in Noah's 600th year, 2nd month and 17th day, the flood started (Gen. 7:4, 11). In the 601st year, 2nd month, 27th day of the month, Noah left the ark (Gen. 7:13). Therefore, they were in the ark one year and ten days, plus the seven days before the flood started, making a total of one year and seventeen days in the ark. One year and ten days after the rain started, the earth was dry.

   e. Gen. 7:19 - All the hills were covered and water rose fifteen cubits above the highest mountain which was twenty to thirty feet above the mountains.

   f. If the flood was local, the Rainbow Covenant has been broken many times, for there have been many local floods (Gen. 9:11-16).

   g. 2 Pet. 3:3-7 - Since the second destruction of the earth will be universal, so was the flood.

   h. Matt. 24:37-39 - Jesus believed in Noah, the ark, and the flood that "took them all away."

8. 2 Pet. 3:5-6 - So I believe in a universal flood and that the "world that then existed perished, being flooded with water."

Verse 8: *By faith Abraham obeyed when he was called to go out to the place which he would receive as an inheritance. And he went out, not knowing where he was going.* Abraham obeyed. It takes great faith to leave one's homeland and go to a place unknown but faith is a conviction of things not seen.

1. Gen. 12:1-4 - Abraham departed to a land that God would show him.

2. Acts 7:1-5; Gen. 12:8-9 - God was to give land to Abraham and his descendants. It was to be their inheritance. This promise was primarily fulfilled in the time of Joshua.

   a. Gen. 12:9 - This land was to be given to Abraham's descendants.

   b. Joshua 21:43-44 - God gave all of it to them.

   c. Joshua 23:15-16 - It was conditional on their being faithful.

3. Acts 7:5 - Since God promised to give it to Abraham himself and to his descendants, the ultimate fulfillment of this promise will be in the "new heaven and new

earth" that He will create for all saints in both the Old and New Testament (Isa. 65:17; 2 Pet. 3:13; Rev. 21-22).

4. Rom. 4:13 - Abraham is the heir of the world but it is the "world to come" that the writer had already referred to in Hebrews 2:5 that Abraham and his descendants will inherit. This inheritance was prepared in the mind of God from the foundation of the world according to Jesus in Matthew 25:34.

Verse 9: *By faith he dwelt in the land of promise as in a foreign country, dwelling in tents with Isaac and Jacob, the heirs with him of the same promise* - Abraham was a sojourner in the land. It appears from this that Abraham never regarded Canaan as his home. Neither he, nor Isaac, nor Jacob ever built a permanent residence in this country. They were satisfied to live in movable tents. Isaac and Jacob were heirs of the same promise. By faith they all knew that God would indeed one day fulfill His promise to them literally.

Verse 10: *for he waited for the city which has foundations, whose builder and maker is God* - Abraham, with an eye of faith, was not considering the land of Canaan his home, as it was, but the antitype of Canaan or heaven. Abraham expected the possession of the Promised Land for himself and his descendants and his faith looked beyond this to the heavenly abode of the righteous. By faith he was convinced of things not seen by him at the time concerning the eternal promised land.

Verse 11: *By faith Sarah herself also received strength to conceive seed, and she bore a child when she was past the age, because she judged Him faithful who had promised* - Sarah was the mother of the faithful since Abraham was the "father of the faithful." Faith sees the invisible, believes the incredible, and receives the impossible, as in Sarah's case.

1. Genesis 18:12-14 - It may seem strange that she is mentioned since she laughed. But all believers have doubts

at various times.
2. Genesis 17:17 - Of course, Abraham laughed at first too.
3. Genesis 21:1-7 - The verses record the birth of Isaac.
4. Genesis 17:17 - Sarah was about ninety years old when Isaac was born.

Verse 12: *Therefore from one man, and him as good as dead, were born as many as the stars of the sky in multitude—innumerable as the sand which is by the seashore* – The one man refers to Abraham. He was "as good as dead" as far as bearing children are concerned. As the stars in the sky are innumerable, so would his descendants be.

1. I understand that there was a time when men did not believe that the stars were innumerable but rather they could be counted. The fact that the Bible says they are innumerable is one sure sign of the inspiration of the Bible.
2. Gen. 12:11; 16:3; 25:6 - Abraham had many physical descendants because he had Sarah and Hagar, as well as concubines. He also has numerous spiritual descendants (Rom. 4).
3. Genesis 25:7 - He lived 175 years. He did have concubines and children by them.

Verse 13: *These all died in faith* - "These all" may not refer to all those that have been mentioned even though all those mentioned from Abel to Sarah did die (or in Enoch's case was translated) in faith. But some think this particular statement was made concerning those who had received the promise, namely, Abraham, Isaac, Jacob, and Sarah.

1. Abel, Enoch, and Noah will receive the benefits of the promise of salvation in Christ as well as access to the heavenly country even though they may have never specifically heard it.
2. Hebrews 11:5 - Enoch did not die.

not having received the promises – That is, not having received
the fulfillment of the promises.

1. Hebrews 11:17 - Abraham had received the promises,
   but not the fulfillment of them.
   a. He never saw his descendants in such large
      numbers.
   b. He never saw his seed receive an inheritance
      in Canaan.
   c. He never saw the earth blessed through his seed.
2. He would personally receive the blessing of the things
   promised at the proper time, but he did not receive
   them during his lifetime on earth. The ultimate fulfillment of the promise will be in the new heavens and new
   earth.

*but having seen them afar off were assured of them, embraced
them* - They really believed the promises would be fulfilled,
though they did not see them fulfilled. They had conviction of
things not seen.

*and confessed that they were strangers and pilgrims on the
earth* - By their actions they confessed that they were strangers here. They were not looking for earthly possessions themselves because they dwelt in tents and never had a permanent
dwelling place on earth.

Verse 14: *For those who say such things declare plainly that
they seek a homeland* - They sought a homeland, a country.

1. Gen. 11:31 - It was neither Canaan nor the country
   Abraham came out of which was Ur of the Chaldeans.
2. He could have returned if that was the country he had
   in mind as stated in the next verse.

Verse 15: *And truly if they had called to mind that country
from which they had come out, they would have had opportunity to return* - This suggests that nothing stood in their way

from going back to the land Abraham came out of if they had wanted to.

Verse 16: *But now they desire a country, that is, a heavenly country* - They desired a country in heaven.

> 1. Hebrews 11:10 - He looked for the city, a heavenly city.
> 2. He looked for a country better than Canaan or Ur of the Chaldeans and better than any earthly country.
> 3. Likely God gave the Patriarchs information about the heavenly country far beyond what is recorded in Genesis.
> 4. Jude 1:14-15 - There were many things prophesied in the Old Testament that are not actually recorded there such as this prophecy of Enoch.

Therefore God is not ashamed to be called their God - God was proud of these Old Testament saints.

> 1. Ex. 3:6 - He said He was their God.
> 2. Matt. 22:23-32 - He is the God of the living.
> 3. Job 1:8 - God was proud of Job and said there were none like him.

for He has prepared a city for them - This probably refers to the same place as John 14:1-2 and other references to heaven.

> 1. 1 Pet. 1:3-5 - Heaven is the inheritance of the saints.
> 2. Isa. 65:17; 2 Pet. 3:13; Rev. 21-22 - Heaven is ultimately the "new heaven and new earth" promised to all saints both in the Old Testament and the New.
> 3. Matt. 25:34 - The kingdom that we will ultimately inherit is the one prepared in the mind of God from the foundation of the world.
> 4. Rev. 13:8 - Christ was slain in the mind of God from the foundation of the world.

Verse 17: *By faith Abraham, when he was tested, offered up*

Isaac, and he who had received the promises offered up his only begotten son - This is recorded in Genesis 22:1-13.

1. "Tested" means put to the test or proved.
   a. Genesis 16:16 - Abraham offered Isaac as a sacrifice.
   b. Genesis 21:12 - In Isaac shall the seed be called.
2. Abraham offered up his only begotten son through whom the promises were to be fulfilled.
   a. It was through Isaac, that Abraham was going to be a great nation and be given the land of Canaan.
   b. It was through the descendants of Isaac, that Christ was going to come and bless all nations and now Abraham is told to kill him.

Verse 18: *of whom it was said, In Isaac your seed shall be called* - How old was Isaac at this time? Adam Clark says he was 33. Josephus said he was 25. Others believe 36. Josephus or Adam Clark could be right. The common Sunday School card presentation of Isaac as a beautiful little boy is probably not right. But really we don't know how old he was, but I would believe he was likely twenty or older. The footnote in the NKJV and the ESV both render him as a "young man."

Verse 19: *concluding that God was able to raise him up, even from the dead* - According to Genesis 22:5, Abraham expected he and Isaac to come back from the sacrifice.

from which he also received him in a figurative sense - He received him back from the altar as one raised from the dead. As far as Abraham was concerned, he was dead because he really intended to kill him and had killed him in his own mind. Therefore he was *figuratively* raised from the dead.

Verse 20: *By faith Isaac blessed Jacob and Esau concerning things to come* - Isaac blessed them by telling them things to come. These were things that Isaac had "not seen" and would

not see except by faith. Yet he still had conviction and assurance that these things would happen

1. Genesis 27:26-29 – He blesses Jacob.
2. Genesis 27:34-40 - He blesses Esau but the descendants of Esau (Edomites) did not prosper as descendants of Jacob in the long run.

Verse 21: *By faith Jacob, when he was dying, blessed each of the sons of Joseph, and worshiped, leaning on the top of his staff* - The account of this is in Genesis 48:1-22.

1. Gen. 48:5 - Jacob counted the sons of Joseph as his own.
2. Gen. 48:14 - Ephraim would be more prominent than Manasseh even though he was younger.
3. Gen. 48:16 - Israel's name was on them and Joseph actually got a double portion in the Promised Land.

Verse 22: *By faith Joseph, when he was dying, made mention of the departure of the children of Israel, and gave instructions concerning his bones.* – In Genesis 50:24-25, Joseph told his brothers to carry his bones out of Egypt and bury them in Canaan. He was *sure* that God would bring them out of Egypt and believed in the things *not seen.*

1. Ex. 13:19 - They took the bones of Joseph when they left.
2. Josh. 24:32 - They buried them in Shechem in the land of Canaan.
3. His coffin would serve to remind Israel of: (a) the *death* of people; (b) the *deliverance* from all problems; and (c) the *dependability* of all promises.

Verse 23: *By faith Moses, when he was born, was hidden three months by his parents, because they saw he was a beautiful child; and they were not afraid of the king's command.* – The account of Moses being born and then hidden is recorded in Exodus 2:1-10. By the providence of God the baby Moses was given to his mother as his nurse. This is no doubt the reason for Moses knowing about God and His people.

1. Ex. 1:8-22 - A new Pharaoh decreed that all male children born to Hebrew women be put to death.
2. Ex. 2:10 - Pharaoh's daughter named him Moses which means "drawn out" because she drew him out of the water.

Verses 24-26 - *By faith Moses, when he became of age, refused to be called the son of Pharaoh's daughter, choosing rather to suffer affliction with the people of God than to enjoy the passing pleasures of sin, esteeming the reproach of Christ greater riches than the treasures in Egypt; for he looked to the reward.* – Because of his faith Moses knew what to refuse and what to choose in order to win and not lose. He chose to suffer affliction with the people of God rather than the affluence in Egypt. He knew sin's pleasure would soon pass, and he knew that his God would reward faithfulness. These verses tell us about the *riches he refused*; the *reproach he received*; and the *reward he respected*.

1. Deut. 34:5-7 - Moses lived 120 years. His life can be divided into three periods of forty years each. He spent forty years in Egypt learning how to be a leader. He spent forty years in the wilderness learning how to survive in the wilderness. Then he spent forty years leading the children of Israel in the wilderness.
2. Matt. 17:1-5; Lk. 9:31 - He was with Elijah and Jesus on the mountain when the appearance of Jesus changed. They were talking about the death of Jesus for sin.
3. 1 Cor. 3:8-9; Rev. 14:13 - Moses looked to the reward and so should we. Our "works" follow us in death because we will be rewarded for them.
4. Matt. 10:40-42 - Jesus notices and rewards us for giving as little as a cup of cold water to the needy because

of our faith in Him.

Verse 27: *By faith he forsook Egypt, not fearing the wrath of the king; for he endured as seeing Him who is invisible.* - In Exodus 10:28-29, we learn that Moses was not afraid of Pharaoh. He faced him head on. Why? He had a conviction concerning Him who is invisible and things "not seen." This takes us back to the definition of faith in verse one.

Verse 28: *By faith he kept the Passover and the sprinkling of blood, lest he who destroyed the firstborn should touch them* - This has reference to the last plague brought on the Egyptians.

1. The Ten Plagues in Exodus:
    a.   Water to blood (7:20)
    b.   Frogs (8:5-6)
    c.   Lice (8:16-17)
    d.   Flies (8:24)
    e.   Cattle dying (9:6)
    f.   Boils (9:10)
    g.   Hail (9:24-25)
    h.   Locusts (10:13)
    i.   Darkness (10:22)
    j.   Death of firstborn (11:1)
2. Ex. 11:5 - The last plague was death of firstborn of both man and beast.
3. Ex. 12:1-14 - To protect Israelites, they were to kill lamb and sprinkle it's blood on doorposts and lintels of houses. God said, "When I see the blood I will pass over you..."
4. Ex. 12:25 - They were to keep the Passover in the land of Canaan. According to Exodus 12:28-31, they did as God commanded.
5. 1 Cor. 5:7 - Christ is our Passover sacrificed for us. We know the firstborn in the house was thankful to have blood on the door and we should be thankful when the blood of Christ is applied to us and spiritual death passes over us.

Verse 29: *By faith they passed through the Red Sea as by dry land, whereas the Egyptians, attempting to do so, were drowned* – This is the Israelites leaving Egypt. When Pharaoh and his army attempted to cross they drowned (Exodus 14:5-9; 15-16; 19-23; 26-28).

1. Ex. 14:30 - God saved Israel that day.
2. 1 Cor. 10:1-2 - They were baptized into Moses. Baptism stood as the dividing line between slavery and freedom.
3. 1 Cor. 10:11 - This is surely a type of our salvation in Christ. These are our examples.
4. Exodus 14:21 - We might not notice that strong winds were involved in parting the sea. The Holy Spirit is compared to wind in the new birth and some do not notice His role (Jn. 3:8).

Verse 30: *By faith the walls of Jericho fell down after they were encircled for seven days* - Jericho was the first city conquered by Israel in the land of Canaan (Josh. 6:1-5, 20).

1. Josh. 6:3 - The Israelites were to go around the walls once a day for six days.
2. Josh. 6:4 - On the seventh day, they were to go around seven times which totals thirteen times during the seven days.

Verse 31: *By faith the harlot Rahab did not perish with those who did not believe, when she had received the spies with peace* - Rahab was a harlot who hid the two spies Joshua sent to spy out Jericho (Joshua 2:1-4).

1. Josh. 2:8-19 - She was told what to do and she did it. He does not commend all that she did but He does commend and reward her faith (Joshua 6:22-23).
2. Jam. 2:25 - She was justified by her faith because her works demonstrated that she believed in the God of Israel.

3. **Matt. 1:5** - Rahab was the mother of Boaz and Boaz was the father of Obed and Obed was the father of Jess, who was the father of David.
   a. **Matt. 1:5** - She was David's great-great grandmother.
   b. **Matt. 1:1-5** - She was one of four women listed in the genealogy of Christ.
4. **Heb. 11:30** - She did not perish with them that believed not. This shows why the Canaanites were destroyed.
5. **Heb. 11:40** - Rahab is in "Faith's Hall of Fame". She went from the "house of shame" to the "hall of fame" because of her faith in things she had "not seen."

Verse 32: *And what more shall I say? For the time would fail me to tell of Gideon* - Gideon was the fifth judge of Israel (Judges 6:11-8:35).

1. **Judges 6-7** - He won a battle against his enemies with three hundred men.
2. **Judges 6:36-40** - He wanted a fleece of wool to have dew on it but he wanted the ground dry. The next day he *"squeezed the fleece together, he wrung the dew out of the fleece, a bowlful of water"* (6:38). Then he wanted the ground wet and fleece dry and it was.

and Barak - Barak was a leader in Israel during the time of Deborah who was the fourth Judge. He led Israel to a victory over the king of Canaan and a man named Sisera. Sisera is the one who had a nail driven through his temples (Judges 4:6-5:12).

and Samson - The thirteenth Judge of Israel (Judges 13:24-16:31). He battled the Philistines, but was mostly remembered for his love for Delilah (Judges 16:4-30).

and Jephthah - He was the ninth Judge of Israel (Judges 11:1-12:7). He defeated the children of Amnon and made a foolish vow that if God would deliver them to him, he would offer whatever came out of his house as a burnt offering on his return. His daughter came out to meet him and he did to her according to his vow (Judges 11:30-40). Some do not think that he actually killed her but it seems to me that he likely did, although I'm not sure.

also of David - He was the second king of Israel. The account of his life is given primarily in first and second Samuel.

1. 1 Sam. 16 - Samuel anoints David. His death is recorded in 1 Kings 2:10-11.
2. 1 Sam. 13:14; Acts 13:22 - He was a man after God's own heart.

and Samuel - He was the fifteenth and last judge. All of Israel from Dan to Beersheba knew that Samuel was established to be a prophet of the Lord, even when he was a boy. (1 Sam. 3:20).

and the prophets – This could be all those in the Old Testament such as Elijah, Elisha, Daniel, Jeremiah, Ezekiel, Hosea, Joel, etc.

Verse 33: *who through faith* - The writer does not mean that all the ones he is about to mention did all the things mentioned, but that some of them did some of the things while others did the others.

subdued kingdoms - This would include David who defeated the Syrians, Edomites, Ammonites, etc. (2 Sam.). Jephthah defeated the Ammonites (Judges 11). Samson defeated the Philistines (Judges 13-16).

worked righteousness - Many of those just mentioned did what was right on various occasions.

obtained promises - "Obtained promises" could mean they obtained verbal promises as Abraham did (Genesis 22:18), or it could mean that they obtained the blessings of the things promised, such as victories and other blessings.

stopped mouths of lions - Daniel is probably the one the writer had in mind (Dan. 6). His faith stopped the mouths of lions because God had shut the lion's mouths (Dan. 6:8 & 22).

Verse 34: *quenched the violence of fire* - During the time of Nebuchadnezzar, three Hebrew children were thrown in the fire because they wouldn't bow down to the image Nebuchadnezzar had made (Dan. 3).

escaped edge of sword - David escaped Goliath's sword (1 Sam. 17:44-51). David escaped Saul's spear more than once (1 Sam. 18:11; 19:10-12). Elisha escaped the sword of the Syrians by striking them blind (2 Kings 6:18).

out of weakness were made strong - Samson could head this list (Judges 16). Hezekiah was made strong after his illness (Isa. 38:1-8).

became valiant in battle, turned to fight the armies of the aliens - The books of Joshua, Judges, Samuel, and Kings supply instances of this in abundance.

Verse 35: *Women received their dead raised to life again* - The widow of Zarephath's son was raised from the dead by Elijah (1 Kgs. 17:9-24). The Shunammite woman's son was raised by the faith of Elisha (2 Kgs. 4:32-37).

Others were tortured, not accepting deliverance - They did not accept deliverance even if/when offered them on condition that they renounce their faith. They had just as much faith as those who were triumphant, yet they were tortured. The idea that faith will make everything go well is clearly refuted by these and many other examples such as Jesus, Paul, and these Hebrew believers as we have already learned (Heb. 10:32-34).

that they might obtain a better resurrection - The better resurrection is the resurrection at the last day. All will be raised
but the faithful will have it far better than unbelievers.

Verse 36: *Still others had trials of mockings* - In Judges 16:25
the Philistines mocked Samson. Job was mocked in Job 19:13-
19. Elisha was mocked by some young people in 2 Kings 2:23-
24.

and scourgings, yes, and of chains and imprisonment - Joseph,
Samson, Micah and numerous others are examples of this
mistreatment.

Verse 37: *They were stoned, they were sawn in two, were tempted, were slain with the sword. They wandered about in sheep-
skins and goatskins, being destitute, afflicted, tormented* - Some
believe Isaiah was sawn in two. Numerous others who had
faith suffered temptation and affliction.

Verse 38: *of whom the world was not worthy. They wandered
in deserts and mountains, in dens and caves of the earth* - The
wicked world did not deserve these good examples of faith in
these men and women.

Verse 39: *And all these, having obtained a good testimony
through faith, did not receive the promise* - All of these obtained a good report because of their faith. But during their
lifetime they did not receive the fulfillment of the promise of
God to bless all nations by the seed of Abraham. Jesus did not
come during their lifetime as He has in ours.

Verse 40: *God having provided something better for us,* - The
better thing that God has provided for us is the new and better covenant with new and better promises (Heb. 8:6). This
includes all the superior blessings that Jesus provides for us.
We have received the fulfillment of the promises of Christ
who has provided for us a new and living way into the presence of God.

1. **Gal 3:26-29 - We belong to Christ and are heirs of the promise God made to Abraham.**
2. **They were not in Christ. They did not belong to Christ because He had not come when they lived. They had no absolute forgiveness of sins and they did not have the blessings we have in Christ.**

that they should not be made perfect apart from us – **Neither their faith nor their absolute forgiveness would be complete without us and the promise that has been fulfilled to us in Christ. They are redeemed and made perfect because of the work of Jesus Christ. Without the work He has done for and to us, they would not be forgiven and blessed as they were then and are now.**

HEBREWS
Chapter Twelve

JESUS IS A SUPERIOR SOURCE
OF ENCOURAGEMENT

Special Note: The men and women in the previous chapter lived by faith and remained faithful to the end. This would encourage the Hebrew believers to do the same. However, *Jesus provides superior encouragement* to any one or all of the witnesses combined. As believers in the New Covenant, we keep "looking to Jesus" because He is the "author and finisher of our faith."

Verse 1: *Therefore* - This ties in with what has been said in chapter eleven.

we also, since we are surrounded by so great a cloud of witnesses - Some think this has reference to games much like that of the ancient Greeks where the spectators in seats that surrounded the stadium watched and cheered on the runners who participated. This cloud of witnesses looking on is supposed to be the Old Testament saints just mentioned by the writer in Hebrews 11, but I believe the cloud of witnesses are those that he had just referred to throughout the preceding chapter and that they witness to us by the faithful lives they lived when they were alive — and not by watching us run now. I do not believe that they are watching us from heaven as we run the Christian race. If it helps some to believe that they are watching us then, that is fine for them, but I do not believe that it is actually true.

1. Would those watching us see us if we stumble? If so, how do you suppose that would affect them?
2. Ecc. 9:5-6 – These verses seem to teach that the dead do not know what's going on under the sun, so can they be

actually watching?

3. It seems to me that they are called witnesses because of the testimony they have borne as to the power and victory of faith they had when they lived.
   a. They witness to us that men can live by faith and please God.
   b. The cloud of witnesses lived by faith and remained faithful to the end. This would encourage the Hebrew believers to do the same.

let us lay aside every weight – The writer is comparing the Christian life here to running in a race. When runners run in a race they do not wear combat boots or suits of armor. They run in as little clothing as necessary and as light as possible.

1. 1 Cor. 9:24-26: Paul on other occasions used a race to illustrate the Christian life (Gal. 2:2; Phil. 2:16; 2 Tim. 2:5).
2. "Every weight" would be anything that would hinder us from living the Christian life faithfully.
   a. In an actual race, you would want to lay aside anything that would hinder or slow you down.
   b. We must do the same in our lives. It may be a hobby, habit, job, business, T.V., relationship, friends, etc.
   c. Anything that hinders must be laid aside (Mark 9:43-48; 2 Cor. 6:14ff).

and the sin which so easily ensnares us - In the context of the Book of Hebrews, it seems that "unbelief" is the sin he has in mind, though the verse would also teach them to lay aside any sin which hinders one from running the Christian race.

1. Heb. 10:39-11:40 - The immediate context indicates that the primary reference is to the sin of unbelief.
2. Heb. 3:12 - An evil heart of unbelief is what they were primarily being warned against.

and let us run with endurance – The faithful life is a life of endurance like those the writer had just discussed in the previous chapter.

1. Heb. 10:36 - They had need of endurance.
2. Heb. 10:24 - Holding fast their confession would require endurance.

the race that is set before us - It is not just any race. It is the race that is set before us. Many times religious people run, but they run in the wrong race.

Verse 2: *Looking to Jesus* - Here he mentions the greatest example of faithfulness and endurance there is.

1. Here he saved the best example of faith for last. He does not put Christ with the faithful in the O.T. He refers to Him above them all as in a person that deserves to stand by Himself.
2. Matt. 14:22-33 - As long as Peter looked to Jesus, he walked on the water but when he saw the wind, he took his eyes off Jesus and began to sink.

the author and finisher of our faith – He is the cause and finisher of our faith. He has begun a good work in us and He will complete it (Phil. 1:6).

who for the joy that was set before Him endured the cross, despising the shame - It was not a joy to suffer and die. It was no "joy" to die on the cross, but it was something He "endured" for the joy of saving man from sin.

1. Heb. 2:10 - He will bring many to glory by His suffering on the cross.
2. Jesus has made the cross famous. We make jewelry in the form of a cross. When we think of the cross, we think of an innocent man dying, but when Christ died

on it, it was regarded as the punishment for the vilest and meanest outlaws and criminals. It was the place for murderers, thieves, and rebels. It had more shame connected with it in that day than the gas chamber, electric chair, or gallows has today. Illustration: Suppose today you asked a man about his brother and he says he was electrocuted in "the chair" in Atmore, AL. Right away you would know he was a criminal, a menace to society and one who in all probability deserved to die for crimes against state. This is the same shame that was connected with the cross when Christ died on it.

3. Phil. 2:5-7 - This will help us understand such statements as "even the death of the cross."
4. Gal. 3:13 - It was not only a horrible way to die, but also had great shame connected with it.

and has sat down at the right hand of the throne of God – As has already been emphasized, Christ is seated at the right hand of God.

1. Acts 2:33 - Peter said He was exalted to the right hand of God.
2. Heb. 1:3 - He sat down at the right hand of the majesty on high.
3. Hebrews 1:8 - He has a throne and scepter which is a ruler's staff or rod held in the hand of kings as a token of authority.

Verse 3: *For consider Him* - They had already considered the heroes of faith in chapter eleven, and now they needed to see what Jesus had endured for them (1 Peter 2:21).

who endured such hostility from sinners - Jesus was opposed and resisted by sinful men. Men contradicted and opposed Him. They were hostile toward Him.

1. John 1:11 - His own nation rejected him.

2. **Ps. 2:2** - The kings of the earth set themselves against the Lord and His Anointed One.

3. If these Jewish Christians would just consider what Jesus endured from sinners, they would not think so much of the persecution they were receiving from their unbelieving brethren, nor be so disheartened by them as to reject or renounce the gospel.

against Himself - What did they say about Him? Among other things they said the following:

1. **Matt. 12:24** - He casts out demons by power of the devil.
2. **Mark 3:21** - They said He was crazy.
3. **Matt. 11:19** - He was called a glutton and a drunkard.
4. **Matt. 22:63** - The leaders said He was a deceiver.

lest you become weary and discouraged in your souls - Discouragement has always been a threat to faith in the church. The Hebrew Christians were having problems with this very thing.

1. **Gal. 6:9** - Be not weary in well doing for in due time we will reap.
2. **1 Cor. 9:24-27** - Men running in a race may get tired and weary after a long run but it is only the one who finishes who will receive the prize. It is the same with the Christian race as Paul clearly reveals.

Verse 4: *You have not yet resisted to bloodshed, striving against sin* – They had not *yet* resisted to bloodshed. The persecution they were suffering had not yet caused them to shed their blood.

1. **Acts 7, 12** - Stephen, James, and numerous others from the Jerusalem church, had shed their blood in times past, but it is only the living members of the Jerusalem church that the writer is talking about.

2. The persons addressed here had not yet been called on to suffer what Christ and many others had to suffer in their fight against sin.

3. The word "yet" may imply that the time was coming when they would be called upon to give their lives in the fight against sin.

    a. Heb. 13:22 - All of this should serve to encourage these Hebrews to remain faithful and not go back to Judaism.

    b. Heb. 12:12 - Some among them were becoming faint of heart and discouraged because of the persecution, trials, and afflictions.

Verse 5: *And you have forgotten the exhortation which speaks to you as to sons: My son, do not despise the chastening of the Lord, nor be discouraged when you are rebuked by Him* – The writer reminds them of a truth stated by Solomon that applies at all times and in all places as he quotes Proverbs 3:11-12.

1. Prov. 3:11-12 - The fact that Paul quotes this here, in this context, proves that the burdens that these saints were suffering is actual proof of God's love, not evidence of His indifference.

2. Some were evidently thinking, "Well, God doesn't care anything about us or we would not be persecuted like we are."

3. Because of this attitude the writer reminded them of this truth:

    a. They had forgotten the word of encouragement found in Proverbs, which says that God disciplines and corrects His children.

    b. They shouldn't lose heart when rebuked by Him. There is profit in discipline.

Verse 6: *For whom the Lord loves He chastens, And scourges every son whom He receives* - Whom the Lord loves He disciplines or trains. It is like a good football coach who trains and disciplines his players.

1. Rev. 3:19 - Those He loves He chastens. Therefore training is proof of His love for us.
2. God is a good Coach because He knows how to train, which includes discipline.

Verse 7: *If you endure chastening, God deals with you as with sons* - If they were called upon to suffer, God was dealing with them as sons.

for what son is there whom a father does not chasten - It is a characteristic of a good earthly father to train his children by discipline and correction. Therefore, it should not shock us or make us think less of God if He does what any good parent would and should do.

1. Prov. 22:6 - When we train our children in the way they should go it is proof of our love and concern for their well-being.
   a. Indifference and failure to discipline or train them only shows that we don't really love them as we should.
   b. These Hebrews needed to know that the hardships and persecutions God was allowing them to endure was proof of His love.
2. God sends and/or allows persecution in order to help His children stay close to Him.
3. Hab. 1:5-11 - Many times in the Old Testament God sent nations to punish and discipline His people in order to get them to repent and keep them from going further into idolatry and rebellion.
4. Job 2:3-7 - However, it can be said that God does something when in reality He only allows it. This could be the case with the Hebrew Christians.

Verse 8: *But if you are without chastening, of which all have become partakers, then you are illegitimate and not sons* - If we are without chastisement or training, we are illegitimate children and not true sons. If God did not discipline and correct us it would be proof that we are not true children of God.

Verse 9: *Furthermore, we have had human fathers who corrected us, and we paid them respect. Shall we not much more readily be in subjection to the Father of spirits and live* - Our human fathers corrected us and we respected and obeyed them and loved them. This is part of training. God is the Father of our spirits and because of that He trains us.

1. Zech. 12:1 - God is called the Father of Spirits because He forms the spirit in man.
2. Heb. 10:36 - We need endurance in order to receive the promise of eternal life.

Verse 10: *For they indeed for a few days chastened us as seemed best to them, but He for our profit* - Our earthly parents disciplined and corrected us or trained us for just a little while as they thought best, though they may at times have been wrong. However, God's training is always for our good. God will never ever discipline us just because He has power or just to show that He can, or because He enjoys seeing His people disciplined. It is always for our profit, not for punishment.

that we may be partakers of His holiness - His discipline is to make us what we ought to be, that is, that we might be made holy. He trains us to be holy because He knows that is the best way to live.

1. 2 Cor. 12:7-10 - God allowed Satan to inflict Paul in some way for his own good to keep him humble.
2. James 1:2 - The trying of our faith produces patience.
3. 2 Cor. 4:17 - Our light affliction works for us a far more exceeding and eternal weight of glory.
4. Psalm 119:67, 71 - Affliction at times helps us to do right.
    a. God sometimes allows persecution and affliction to come on His children and is to be regarded

as divine training as it was in the case of these
Hebrew Christians.

    b. Luke 1:6 - Zacharias was righteous and blameless
but not nearly perfect as he was not able to speak
because of the sin of unbelief (Lk. 1:20).

5. Romans 5:3 - We can glory in tribulation because tribulation produces patience or endurance.

6. Amos 4:6-12 - God brought affliction on Israel in order
to get them to repent, but they refused.

7. Hag. 1:5-11 - God disciplined His people in Haggai's
day because they would not work on the temple as He
directed.

Verse 11: *Now no chastening seems to be joyful for the present,
but painful; nevertheless, afterward it yields the peaceable fruit
of righteousness to those who have been trained by it* – Discipline or intense training is not joyous but painful. When a
good football coach has his team in training or practice it can
hurt because no discipline seems pleasant at the time it is ad-
ministered. It is actually painful. However, afterward when
they are in a real game it will help them play well and It is
the same way with God's training of us because it is designed
to produce the fruit of righteousness for those who have been
trained by it.

1. When we discipline and correct our children, it is not
a joyous occasion for them, but painful. However, later
on it makes them what they ought to be if it has the
effect on them that was intended.

2. I'm not suggesting that all suffering done by Christians is to be considered divine discipline, but it can be
a form of training.

    a. It was discipline in the case of those Hebrews or
the writer's point is meaningless.

    b. And, no doubt, it is the case in many instances
today.

3. Divine discipline is not the only cause of suffering. For
example:

a. Some suffer because of sin of others - drunk drivers, etc.
b. Some suffer because of their own sins - King Saul.
c. Some suffer as result of God's providence working in the affairs of men to fulfill his purpose - Joseph.
d. Some suffer as a result of testing to which man is subjected - Job.
e. Some suffering is because one is a Christian (John 16:33).

NOTE: One cannot always know the cause of his suffering. It could be because of any of these things or others I haven't mentioned. But beyond question, at times, and perhaps most of the time, it is the discipline/training of God. If Christians never had any tribulation, heartache, persecution, etc. we would not see our need for God. Persecution, distress, etc. is used by the Lord to train those who are His, whether this persecution is sent by Him or whether He just allows it and uses it for the Christian's good. I may not know which it is, but the lesson is the same either way. Hebrews 12:4-11 teaches that God chastens His children. Revelation 3:19 reminds us that it is because of love that He chastens us and it is for our ultimate good. Romans 8:28 says, "For we know that all things work together for good to those who love God..." What are those "things" that work for our good? In the context of Romans 8 it is things like sufferings (Rom 8:18) including tribulation, persecution, famine, sword, etc. (Rom. 8:35).

Verse 12: *Therefore strengthen the hands which hang down, and the feeble knees* - In view of the fact that the persecutions and afflictions are designed as the training of the Lord and are for our profit, then that should be encouraging rather than disheartening. Instead of proving that God did not care for us, they proved rather that He was dealing with them as any good Father would do for His children.

1. Heb. 12:1 - In verse one of this chapter the writer compares the Christian life to a race and here he seems to still have that figure in mind. Some of them were wearied and exhausted in their Christian race because of the persecutions, troubles, etc. They were suffering which was the reason for the feeble knees. Here is a picture of weary runners who are told to take courage and make every effort to bear up under the trials they were enduring.
2. 2 Tim. 4:7 - Like Paul they must finish the race.

Verse 13: *and make straight paths for your feet, so that what is lame may not be dislocated, but rather be healed* - A race still seems to be in his mind and he says they were to try to clear the obstacles out of the way that were causing them to stumble and fall. This passage likely means that everything should be removed which would hinder anyone (lameness, weariness, weakness, etc.) from running the Christian race. Make paths smooth so the lame would not be turned away, but healed.

Verse 14: *Pursue peace with all people* - The context here requires us to understand this mainly of persecutors. He exhorts them to manifest a spirit of kindness toward all men, even though some were engaged in persecuting them. We are to make war with sin, but not with men.

1. Romans 12:18 - This admonition is to be understood in light of all that is said on the subject. Paul told the Romans to live at peace with all men *if* it is possible.
2. Matt. 5:44 - Jesus said, "Love your enemies..."
3. This does not mean that we will have the same love and affection for them as we do our wives, children, brethren, or friends, but it means to do good to them and help them when and if we can.
4. Rom. 12:19-20 - Like Jesus, Paul teaches not to seek personal vengeance but help those who are our enemies and God will take care of the rest.

5. Gal. 6:10; 1 Thess. 5:14-15; 2 Cor. 9:13; 1 Tim. 2:1 - We are to do good, pray for, and help all men as we have the opportunity to do so.

and holiness, without which no one will see the Lord - Holiness is an important Biblical and Christian theme. Our goal or aim in life is to be holy in word and deed. It is only those who seek to be holy that will see the Lord in peace.

1. 1 Peter 1:16 - We are to seek to be holy but we will never be sinless or even close to perfect in our conduct.
2. Heb. 3:1 - Paul called these Hebrews "holy brethren," yet they were weak, discouraged (12:12), and had not grown as they should (5:12). Nevertheless, they were still holy because of what Jesus had done for them.
3. John 3:3-5 - Illustrates that the word "see" is sometimes used in sense of entering into a welcomed relationship.
4. All will probably see God at judgment, but only the holy will see Him in peace.
5. Only the righteous see Him in peace. To see Him is to dwell with Him, or to see Him in the sense of entering into a welcomed relationship with Him

Verse 15: *Looking carefully* - We are to be looking diligently, and he lists four kinds of troubles to be looking for:

1. Lest any man fail the grace of God.
2. Lest any root of bitterness springing up trouble you.
3. Lest there be any fornicators.
4. Lest there be any profane person.

lest anyone fall short of the grace of God - They must pay close attention and look diligently lest any of them miss the divine favor of God by having an evil heart of unbelief in departing from God (Heb. 3:12).

1. 1 Cor. 9:27; 10:12 - Paul knew he could fall short.

2.   2 Cor. 6:1 - We can receive the grace of God in vain.
3.   Gal. 5:4 - We can fall from grace.

lest any root of bitterness springing up cause trouble, and by this many become defiled - Some think this is a reference to Deuteronomy 29:18 and that it refers to some person in the church who would rise up and cause bitterness and strife among the members. This may be right of course, but it may also have reference to the bitterness that might spring up in the hearts of these Hebrews against those who were persecuting them. If they harbored these bitter feelings against their enemies, they could be defiled by the bitterness. This seems to me to be the meaning.

Verse 16: *lest there be any fornicator or profane person like Esau, who for one morsel of food sold his birthright* - Some understand "fornicator" to mean physical fornication and believe he is talking about one who commits the physical act of fornication like the man in 1 Corinthians 5:1. But this could be talking about spiritual fornication as with those in Revelation 2:20-22 or James 4:4. Profane is the opposite of sacred. A profane person is one who does not properly regard God. Esau treated the birthright with abuse, irreverence, and contempt because he sold it for one morsel of meat. The Hebrew brethren could do the same thing by rejecting the blessings in Christ for earthly comforts.

1.   Romans 7:11-4 - Christians are separated from the Law of Moses in order to be married to Christ. If those who are married to Christ go back to the Law of Moses as these Hebrews were being tempted to do, then they would be committing spiritual fornication and this might be the meaning here.
2.   Genesis 25:29-34 - Esau had been hunting and was tired and weary. Because of his disdain for spiritual things he sold his birthright for one bowl of stew. His most valuable possession was sold for one meal. The

entire honor that is now associated with the name "Jacob" would have been Esau's, but he sold it for one moment's pleasure. He was truly a profane person. The honor Esau parted with can be easily understood by looking at the honors which were bestowed on Jacob.

3. These Hebrews could sell their greatest possession, which is salvation in Christ, for worldly advantages being offered them by returning to Judaism.

Verse 17: *For you know that afterward, when he wanted to inherit the blessing, he was rejected, for he found no place for repentance, though he sought it diligently with tears* - The blessing that Isaac pronounced on Jacob is here referred to. The blessing must have been part of the birthright and the blessing must have been part of what he had sold (Gen. 27:36-38). Isaac could not change his mind once the blessing was given to Jacob, even though Esau would beg him with tears.

1. There was no place for repentance in the mind of Isaac and no way to change his mind.
   a. It does not mean that Esau earnestly sought to repent and could not, but that when once the blessing had been pronounced by his father, it was impossible to change it. The decision was final.
   b. Esau wanted to change the purpose of his father, but it could not be done even with tears and begging.
2. The lesson here seems to be that if these Hebrews, because of some worldly advantage or pleasure of the moment, renounced the gospel system of religion and went back to Judaism, they could not get God to change His mind about salvation being only in Christ no matter how hard they tried.
   a. God's plan of salvation is the gospel and if they go back to Judaism, He is not going to change his mind about it just as Isaac did not and could not change his mind concerning the blessing.

   b. If they sold out and went back to Judaism, there
      would be no more hope for them to be saved than
      there was for Esau to receive the blessing.

NOTE: Hebrews shows that the Gospel is superior to Judaism. The examples of faith in Hebrews 11 and Christ in chapter 12, along with discipline/training is proof of God's love as
their suffering was indeed discipline/training. Also, if they
went back, there would be no hope of being saved. What a
book of encouragement this is!

NOTE: In Hebrews 12:18-29, he compares the law and the
gospel. He compares Judaism with the kingdom of Christ or
the earthly mountain with the heavenly mountain. The reason this book was written was to prevent apostasy and to do
this, the writer now shows that apostasy is more dangerous
under the New Covenant than it was under the Old Covenant. The privileges and responsibilities under the New are
far superior to those of the Old, and therefore the responsibility to be faithful to Jesus is far superior to that of Judaism
and the law of Moses. Not only that, but Judaism was going to
be removed and only Christianity would remain. This would
surely help these Hebrews to remain faithful.

Verse 18: *For* - This word connects this verse with what has
just been said - that is, they should look diligently.

   1.   Lest you fail the grace of God.
   2.   Lest any root of bitterness spring up and trouble you.
   3.   Lest there be any fornicator or profane person.
   4.   *For* your privileges and position under the gospel are
        far superior to those of Judaism.

you have not come to the mountain that may be touched - This
was Mount Sinai and the Old Covenant that was given from
it. It was a mountain that *could* be touched, although at the
giving of the law, the Israelites were not allowed to touch it. It

is here referred to as a mount that might be touched to show
it was a touchable material, or earthly mountain.

1. Ex. 19:12-13 - They could not touch the Mount.
2. These Hebrews had not come to Mount Sinai as the
Israelites had but had come to one superior, as will be
seen later.

and that burned with fire - Mount Sinai burned with fire at the
giving of the law.

1. Ex. 19:18 - God descended in fire.
2. Deut. 4:11 - The Mountain burned with fire.

and to blackness and darkness and tempest - This was more of
the scary stuff that kept them away from God and His presence on the mountain.

Verse 19: *and the sound of a trumpet and the voice of words,
so that those who heard it begged that the word should not be
spoken to them anymore* - God spoke in an audible voice when
He first gave the Ten Commandments to Israel.

1. Ex. 19:19 - There was the sound of a trumpet.
2. Ex 20:1-20 - God spoke the Ten Commandments
to Israel first and they asked that God not speak
to them anymore (Ex. 20:18-19).
3. Deut. 4:12-13 - These verses show that He spoke the
Ten Commandments first and later wrote them down.
4. Deut. 5:22 - He *spoke* the Ten Commandments with a
great voice and He wrote them on two tablets of stone.
5. Deut. 9:9-12 - These verses show that God wrote on
the stones the things which he had *spoken* to them
earlier.
6. Deut. 9:12 - They had turned aside from the way
God had commanded them. When had He command
ed them not to make an image? Answer: He had
spoken the Ten Commandments to Israel before

Moses went upon the mountain to receive them in writing.

Verse 20: *For they could not endure what was commanded* - The meaning is that the manner in which they were communicated inspired terror which they could not bear (Deut. 5:24-25).

And if so much as a beast touches the mountain, it shall be stoned or shot with an arrow - It was such a terrifying situation that even if a beast touched the mount it was to be killed. If man touched the mount, he was to be killed (Ex. 19:13).

Verse 21: *And so terrifying was the sight that Moses said, I am exceedingly afraid and trembling* - It was such a terrible sight that even Moses said, "I exceedingly fear and tremble."

1. This statement of Moses is nowhere recorded in the Old Testament, but there is no doubting that he said it.
    a. Jn. 14:26; 16:13 - The Hebrew writer was obviously guided in what he wrote by the Holy Spirit. Hence, there is no doubt that Moses made this statement, although it is not recorded.
    b. Eph. 3:3-5 - If Paul did not write the Book of Hebrews, then a prophet or one of the other apostles did, and they too were guided by the Spirit in what they wrote
2. Ex. 19:19 - Some think this statement may have been what Moses spoke here. This may be, but it is just an opinion.
3. These Hebrew Christians had not come to such a terrible manifestation of the presence of God. They had not come to a situation that struck only fear in their hearts. They had not come to a situation where they were shaking in their shoes for fear. But they had come to something far superior to the manifestation that God made at the giving of the law. They had come to a new and living way by which they could draw near to

God in full assurance of faith. (Heb. 10:20-22).

Verse 22: *But you have come to Mount Zion and to the city of the living God, the heavenly Jerusalem,* - As Christians, they had not come to the terrible sights of Mount Sinai, but to the church or the place where the living God dwells, the Heavenly Jerusalem as compared to the earthly one of Judaism.

1. They had already come to Mount Zion, to the city of the Living God, the Heavenly Jerusalem, to the innumerable company of angels, to the general assembly and church of the firstborn. I understand all of these phrases to be referring to the church. In other words, it seems to me that Mount Zion, the city of the living God and the heavenly Jerusalem are all speaking of the church.
2. In the Old Testament, Mount Zion is one of the hills of Jerusalem.
3. The name Zion was sometimes extended to include the whole of Jerusalem.
4. He could be referring to Mount Zion here because the church began in Jerusalem (Mount Zion) instead of Mount Sinai.
    a. Isaiah 2:2-3 - In the Old Testament Mount Zion was associated with the establishment of the church.
    b. Joel 2:32 - Mount Zion is here associated with the outpouring of the Spirit and the establishment of the Lord's church. In Isaiah 2:3 and Joel 2:32, Mount Zion could be referring to the *church*. If so, then Mount Zion is just another descriptive term for the church of our Lord.
5. The city of the living God or the heavenly Jerusalem is identified in the next verse as the "church of the firstborn."
    a. Rev. 21:9-10 – The glorified church here is referred to as a *city*, the *heavenly Jerusalem.*
    b. It is the spiritual dwelling place of God, as com-

pared to the earthly Jerusalem of Judaism.

c. In the Book of Revelation, we have the destruction of the earthly Jerusalem (Rev. 17) but the church, the Lamb's wife, is pictured as the victorious heavenly Jerusalem or the city where the living God dwells.

d. Gal. 4:26 - Paul here refers to the church as the "Jerusalem which is above," or the *heavenly Jerusalem,* when he compares the two covenants to Hagar and Sarah.

to an innumerable company of angels - That there are angels who are present and who watch over and minister to those in the church cannot be seriously denied. In Hebrews 1:14, the writer had already stated that angels are ministering spirits who minister to those who inherit salvation. When we are in the church of our Lord we are in the presence of an innumerable company of angels.

1. Dan. 12:1 – The angel Michael stood watch over God's people in the O.T.
2. Rev. 1:20 – There were angels over each of the seven churches in Asia.
3. 1 Cor. 11:10 – Angels are present in the assemblies of the saints.

Verse 23: *to the general assembly and church of the firstborn* - I am told that the word "firstborn" here is plural and is the same as the word used in Hebrews 11:28, and is surely plural there. Are Christians here called the firstborn (ones)? Just like the firstborn among the Jews had special privileges, so do we as Christians. This could be the meaning here. However, the word is used several other times in the New Testament where it refers to Christ such as Matthew 1:25; Luke 2:7; Romans 8:29 and Colossians 1:15-18. Considering this, the verse could be talking about Christ as the firstborn and not the firstborn ones. Either way would be true.

who are registered in heaven - If he is explaining who the "firstborn" ones are here, then the firstborn ones are Christians who have their names written in the Lamb's book of life.

1. Luke 10:20 - The names of all of the righteous are in the Book of Life.
2. Phil. 4:3 - These two women had their names in the book of life.
3. Rev. 13:8; 21:27 - Those who will be in heaven have their names in the Lamb's book of life.
4. Rev. 3:5 - We must overcome the world or else our names will be blotted out of that book. In Revelation 12:11 we are told how to overcome.
5. Rev. 20:15 - Those whose names are not in the Book of Life at the judgement will be lost.

to God the Judge of all - They had come to God who is the judge of all men.

1. Genesis 18:25 - Abraham referred to Him as the judge of all earth.
2. John 5:22 - Here we learn that although He is the judge of all, He has committed all judgment to the Son.
3. Acts 17:31 - God will judge the world by Jesus Christ.
4. Matt. 25:31 - The Son of Man will be on the throne of judgment when He comes again.

to the spirits of just men made perfect - This may refer to the departed saints of the Old Testament and those who had died already under the New. The saints who die are in a state of perfection where there is no Satan or sin but only salvation.

Verse 24: *To Jesus the Mediator of the new covenant* - Moses was the mediator of the Old Covenant, but these Christians had come to Jesus Christ who is the mediator of the New Covenant. He had already shown in chapter three of this book that Jesus was superior to Moses.

1. Gal. 3:19 - The Old Covenant was appointed by angels in the hand of a mediator.
2. 1 Tim. 2:5 - Jesus is now the only mediator between God and man. If these Hebrew Christians went back to Judaism and rejected Jesus, they would be rejecting the only mediator between God and man.
3. Heb. 9:15 - The writer had already referred to Jesus as the mediator of the New Covenant.

and to the blood of sprinkling - The blood of sprinkling is the blood of Jesus. This simply means that as the blood of animals was sprinkled on the book and people to dedicate the Old Covenant and as the blood of animals was sprinkled on the mercy seat to atone for the sins of Israel, so the blood of Jesus is the means of the New Covenant that has redeemed us from sin.

1. Hebrews 9:18, 19 - Moses dedicated the Old Covenant by sprinkling blood on the book and people.
2. Lev. 16:14, 15 - Blood was sprinkled on the mercy seat by the High Priest on the Day of Atonement.
3. 1 Peter 1:2 - Peter refers to the sprinkling of the blood of Jesus Christ that cleanses us from sin.

that speaks better things than that of Abel – Abel's blood cried out for vengeance whereas the blood of Jesus speaks of grace, mercy and peace.

1. Gen. 4:10 - Abel's blood cried out from the ground for vengeance and vindication.
2. Rom. 5:1 - The blood of Jesus justifies us so that we now have peace with God.
3. Rom. 5:9-10 - Christ's blood cries out for reconcilation with His enemies.

Verse 25: *See that you do not refuse Him who speaks. For if* *they did not escape who refused Him who spoke on earth, much more shall we not escape if we turn away from Him who speaks from heaven* - As stated in the first part of this letter, God has spoken to us by His Son (Heb. 1:1-3). Jesus is our prophet, priest and king and is superior to everything the Hebrews held dear which is what this entire book is about and is what the writer had already proven. There is no escaping judgment if they turn away from the salvation He offers.

1. Heb. 2:1-4 - How shall we escape if we neglect so great a salvation? There is no escape.
2. Heb. 10:26-31 - The writer had already said that those who despised Moses' law died without mercy. He had also warned them concerning more severe punishment for those who despise and reject His salvation.

Verse 26: *whose voice then shook the earth* - This refers to verse nineteen and the time when the voice of God shook the earth at Mount Sinai.

but now He has promised, saying, Yet once more I shake not only the earth, but also heaven - This promise is found in Haggai 2:6. His prophesy was concerning the "Desire of All Nations" who would fill the temple and bring peace to His people.

1. The shaking of the earth and heaven is language God has used over and over to refer to the destruction of nations.
   a. Isaiah 13:1-13 - In reference to the fall of Babylon, God said, "Therefore I will shake the heavens, and the earth shall remove out of her place..."
   b. Matt. 24:29 - Referring to the fall of Jerusalem, Jesus said, "The powers of the heavens shall be shaken..." (Mark 13:25).
2. Heb. 12:26 - This describes a shaking up of the heavens and earth. This is, of course, figurative language denoting the shaking up and destruction of a nation as

in Isaiah 13:13. In this verse, God shows that He was going to remove Judaism by destroying the Jewish Nation in order that that which could not be shaken (the kingdom of Christ) may remain.

Verse 27: *Now this, Yet once more, indicates the removal of those things that are being shaken, as of things that are made, that the things which cannot be shaken may remain* - There are only two things being considered in the context in which this verse is found: Judaism, which originated at the mount that could be touched (12:18), and the church (12:22). Now something is going to be removed in order that something may remain. The writer does not specify what those things are that are going to be removed except to say, "It's those things that are shaken." The thing that cannot be shaken is identified in verse 28 as the kingdom that the Hebrew believers had received. Therefore the things that are "being shaken" are those things relating to Judaism that he is discussing in this context. Since there are only two things being considered - the covenant at Sinai and the kingdom of Christ - and one of these was going to be removed, while the other was going to remain, it seems obvious that those things that are shaken and that were going to be removed, were those things relating to Judaism (the temple, animal sacrifices, priests, etc.).

1. Heb. 8:13 - The Old Covenant was about to vanish away totally and for good with the destruction of the Jewish temple.
2. Hebrews 10:37- This is in keeping with what he had taught earlier about coming in judgment on Jerusalem in a little while.
3. 1 Pet. 4:7 - Peter clearly stated, "But the end of all things is at hand..." Peter was the apostle to the Jews (Gal. 2:7).

Verse 28: *Therefore, since we are receiving a kingdom which cannot be shaken, let us have grace, by which we may serve God acceptably with reverence and godly fear* - Judaism with its temple, priests, and sacrifices was going to be taken out of the way for good and the kingdom of Christ was to remain. It would never be moved or taken out of the way as Judaism was about to be. We serve Him with honor or respect that is felt and shown.

1. Daniel 2:44 - The kingdom Daniel foresaw was one "that would never be destroyed" - which is the same as saying it "cannot be shaken."
2. Daniel 7:13-14 - This kingdom of Daniel is the same as the one these Hebrew Christians had received.
3. Lk. 1:32-33 - Jesus will reign over His kingdom (house of Jacob) forever.
4. Dan. 7:18 - The saints possess the kingdom forever, even forever and ever.
5. 2 Pet. 1:11 - There is the first (primary) phase of the kingdom which is on this present earth and the second (ultimate) phase of the kingdom which will be in the new heaven and new earth (2 Pet. 3:13).

Verse 29: *For our God is consuming fire* - This applies to the willfully disobedient who continue sinning willfully by rejecting the Lord Jesus Christ. God is a caring Father to the faithful, but He is a consuming fire to those who have an evil heart of unbelief and depart from God (Heb. 3:12).

1. Romans 11:22 - We must behold the goodness and severity of God.
2. Heb. 10:31 - It is a fearful thing to fall into the hands of the living God unprepared.

HEBREWS
Chapter Thirteen

JESUS ESTABLISHES A SUPERIOR RELATIONSHIP

Special Note: In this chapter, they are encouraged to be faithful to their Christian responsibilities and duties. As Christians, we realize we are not saved by works that we accomplish (Eph. 2:8-9; Titus 3:3-5), yet in this chapter, Christians are encouraged to be faithful to their responsibilities in being followers of Jesus. There is a major difference in working from salvation and in working for it. We are saved *for* good works but not *by* them. In other words, we are "created in Christ" when we are born again and because we are saved, we seek to serve. We are His "workmanship" because we are in Him, but we are not workmen who work our way into Him. We don't need any muscle and shovel to be saved. But because of His mercy and salvation we seek to do His will in our daily walk. Having shown that Christianity is superior to Judaism in every way, having told them that Judaism is going to be removed and only the kingdom of Christ would remain, the writer now encourages them to be faithful to Christ and their Christian duties. The *superior relationship that has been emphasized throughout the book brings some serious responsibilities.*

Verse 1: *Let brotherly love continue* - Love was one of their strong points (Heb. 6:10). They had not grown in knowledge as they should have, according to Hebrews 5:12, but they did love the brethren. Therefore he now admonishes them to continue this great quality. He did not say let brotherly love *commence*, but let brotherly love *continue*.

    1. John 13:34, 35 - This is the badge of discipleship. It is the mark of being a disciple of Christ.
    2. John 3:18 - Love must be in *deed* and *truth*, not just in

word and tongue.

3. 1 John 3:14 - One way to know we have life is because we love our brethren.

4. 1 Peter 1:22 - We are to see to it that we love one another with a pure heart and fervently.

5. 1 Cor. 13:4-8 - These are the characteristics of brotherly love.

Verse 2: *Do not forget to entertain strangers, for by so doing some have unwittingly entertained angels* - That is why we are to show hospitality to strangers. We are to do good to all men as we have opportunity (Gal. 6:10). Entertaining angels unknowingly may be an illusion to Abraham and Lot who did entertain angels and probably didn't know it *at first.*

1. Gen. 18:1-8 - Abraham entertained angels.

2. Gen. 19:1-11 - So did Lot, but I do not believe that they knew they were angels when they first appeared to them as men.

3. Heb. 1:14 - There may be angels who appear to us in the form of men as they did then. Therefore it is important to show hospitality to all we meet.

4. Gal. 6:10 - Here Paul shows that Christians are to do good to *all men* (strangers included) as we have opportunity.

Verse 3: *Remember the prisoners as if chained with them - those who are mistreated - since you yourselves are in the body also* - In this verse, he is not talking about common criminals who are a menace to society and their fellowman, but the reference here is to those who were in jail for the cause of Christ. This does not mean that we should not help those who are criminals because we should as we have opportunity. But the reference here is to those "in the body" who had been imprisoned for their faith in Jesus.

1. Hebrews 10:34 - This verse shows that the Hebrew writer had been helped as a prisoner. If the alternate

rendering is the correct one, then the Hebrew Christians had helped others who had been in chains.

2. Heb. 13:3 - Here the writer reminds them to remember prisoners. The thing to keep in mind is that the early church received severe persécution. The Jews and the Romans persecuted believers in the first century church at various times and even cast some of them into prison.

3. Acts 8:1; Acts 12; Rev. 1:9 - Believers were persecuted and imprisoned.

4. Heb. 10:34 - The writer himself (whom I believe was Paul) was in chains at this time and most likely Timothy had just been released from prison (Heb. 13:23).

5. Matt. 25:35-45: Those who are accepted by Christ at the judgment are those who visited saints in prison.

6. I believe that we need to do good to those in prison as we have opportunity, but this and other related passages which say or imply that we are to *"Remember the prisoners as if chained with them"* cannot be interpreted to refer to hoodlums, gangsters, racketeers, murderers, rapists, child molesters etc., but to Christians bound for the cause of Christ.

7. 1 Cor. 12:26 – Paul taught that when one member of the body suffers, all are to suffer with them and this would include prisoners (Gal. 6:2; Rom. 12:15).

Verse 4: *Marriage is honorable among all, and the bed undefiled; but fornicators and adulterers God will judge* - This verse clearly states that marriage is an honorable relationship to be in and that sex in marriage is pure and undefiled. All sex outside the bond of marriage is wrong and is condemned by God.

1. Gen. 2:18 - God said here that it is *not good* for man to be alone. This is the general rule to which there have been and are exceptions.

2. Matt. 19:11-12 - Some do not need to be married and being single is good for them. Paul was single and

wished others were (1 Cor. 7:7). However, only those who have the "gift" to be single should remain unmarried. The rest need a companion.

3. 1 Tim. 5:14 - Paul on other occasions taught that younger women *should* marry unless of course they are called and gifted to be single.
4. 1 Tim. 4:1-5 - Forbidding people to marry is the doctrine of the demons and those who teach people not to marry have departed from the faith.
5. Gal. 5:19-21; 1 Cor. 6:9 - These are two of the many passages that teach that fornication and adultery are sinful.

Verse 5: *Let your conduct be without covetousness* - This refers to the love of money. There is a lot said about covetousness and the love of money in the New Testament (1 Tim 6:10; Luke 12:15). Covetousness is an excess desire for wealth or possessions resulting in one being greedy and grasping for wealth. Some are more interested in making money than they are serving God but we cannot serve God and money (Matt. 6:24).

Be content with such things as you have - They were not to be content with where they were as they were admonished to go unto perfection (Heb. 6:1), but they were to be content with what they *had*.

1. This verse does not teach that we shouldn't ever try to improve ourselves or our status in life (Eph. 4:28), but it does mean that we are to be satisfied in whatever condition we find ourselves when it comes to "things."
2. Phil. 4:11-13 - Contentment is something we learn and can practice through Christ who gives us strength. Paul was in prison when he wrote this, but he had learned that happiness did not depend on external circumstances, but on a right relationship with God.

For He Himself has said I will never leave you nor forsake you – This is taught in both the Old Testament and the New.

1. Deut. 31:6, 8; Joshua 1:5 - He had said it on more than one occasion in the Old Testament. He never forsakes the faithful.
2. Deut. 31:16, 17 - However, when the Israelites forsook Him and worshipped and served other gods, then God did forsake them. His promise "not to forsake" is *always* conditional and based on the fact that we continue trusting in Jesus for salvation.
3. 2 Chron. 15:2; 24:20 - These verses show that if God's people forsake Him, then He will forsake them.
4. Heb. 3:12 - These Hebrews were warned against departing from God.
5. Matt. 28:20 - Jesus promised to be with us always even to the end of the age.

Verse 6: *So we may boldly say The LORD is my helper; I will not fear. What can man do to me?* - This is something Christians should be bold and confident about. Since God has promised never to forsake us, we need to confidently say that He will help us. These Hebrews needed to hear this because they were being persecuted at the time because of their faith.

1. Romans 8:31 - Paul made a similar statement here.
2. Yesterday God helped me. Today He will do the same. How long will this continue? Forever praise His name.

Verse 7: *Remember those who rule over you, who have spoken the word of God to you, whose faith follow, considering the outcome of their conduct* - In 1 Tim. 5:17, Paul identifies the "Elders" in the church as those who rule. Since they are the only ones who have the rule over us, this verse must surely be referring to them. More will be said about them and our responsibility to them when we get to verse seventeen of this chapter. Here we are told to "remember" them and here the thing he wanted the Hebrews to remember was the manner of life that they had lived.

1. 1 Tim. 3:1-7; Titus 1:5-9 - The qualifications for Elders are given here.
2. 1 Peter 5:3 - Elders are to be examples for the flock to follow.
3. 1 Pet. 5:1-4; Eph. 4:11 - They are shepherds and pastors who are to lead by example.

Verse 8: *Jesus Christ is the same yesterday, today, and forever -* He is the unchanging Christ. He does not change in His:

1. Ability to aid and relieve those who are tempted (Hebrews 2:18).
2. Interest in saving the lost (Luke 19:10).
3. Ability to save (Hebrews 7:25).
4. Ability to change lives (1 Cor. 6:20-22).
5. Willingness to help (Heb.13:5; Phil. 4:13).
6. Attitude toward error and hypocrisy (Matt. 7:15; 23:1-36)

NOTE: This verse does not say or teach that Jesus is doing the same things He has done before. For example, He's not laying in a manger in Bethlehem (Matt. 2). He's not walking on the earth as He once was. He is obviously not working miracles as He did while He was on earth or even in the early church when the word was being revealed and confirmed (Mk. 16:17-20). This is not to say that He does not work miracles when He pleases (Ps. 115:3), but it is to say that He is not doing them now in the quantity or regularity that He was then.

Verse 9: *Do not be carried about with various and strange doctrines. For it is good that the heart be established by grace, not with foods which have not profited those who have been occupied with them -* He warns them against false teaching and deception. He urges them to trust in the grace of God revealed in the gospel (Acts 20:32; Acts 14:23; John 1:17). Hearts established by grace do not need to rely on dietary rules and legalism. From this passage we see that the gospel emphasis is always on *grace.*

1. Hebrews 12:15 - The writer had urged them not to fall short of the *grace* of God.
2. Acts 20:32 - The gospel message is the "word of His grace." This is not to say that there was no grace in the Old Testament because there surely was (Gen. 6:8).
3. Gal. 1:6-9 - Paul warns against being moved away from the "grace of Christ" to another message.
4. Gal. 5:4 - Those who seek to be justified by law-keeping fall from grace.
5. Heb. 13:9a - The strange doctrine that God warns against in this context would be a message that is graceless. The various and strange doctrines in this verse likely refer to the Judaizing teachers and their doctrine of legalism. While this verse would apply to any false teaching, the context of the book of Hebrews suggests that these "strange doctrines" were being taught by those who were trying to convince these Hebrew Christians to return to Judaism. Also, the reference to "foods" in this verse supports this conclusion (Heb. 9:9-10).

Verse 10: *We have an altar from which those who serve the tabernacle have no right to eat* - The *altar* here is the sacrifice of which Christians eat or partake. Christians do partake of *the sacrifice of Christ.* The question naturally arises: Where did this idea of eating from the altar or partaking of the sacrifices of the altar, come from? Under the Old Covenant, those who served at the altar partook of the sacrifices that were offered on the altar. To eat of the altar was to share in the sacrifice offered on the altar. In the same way, we have an altar to partake or eat of and our altar is the sacrifice of Christ. We are partakers of His sacrifice and we share in the forgiveness His sacrifice brings, but those who serve the tabernacle (those who practice the old law as a means of justification) have no right to the blessings of the sacrifice of Christ because they obviously do not believe in Him.

1. 1 Cor. 9:13 - Paul said that those who minister at the altar are partakers of the offerings.
2. Lev. 6:16; Deut. 18:1 - The priests ate the meat of the sacrifices.

Verse 11: *For the bodies of those animals, whose blood is brought into the sanctuary by the high priest for sin, are burned outside the camp* – Under the Old Covenant the High Priest was to take the blood of a bull and goat and sprinkle it upon the mercy seat for his sins and the sins of the people. But the bodies of those animals were taken outside the camp of Israel and burned.

1. Lev. 16:11-15 - The high priest sprinkled the blood of the sacrifice on the mercy seat for his sins and the sins of the people.
2. Lev. 16:27-28 - The bodies of the calf and the goat were carried outside the camp and burned.

Verse 12: *Therefore Jesus also, that He might sanctify the people with His own blood, suffered outside the gate* - Jesus also suffered outside the gate. The gate here refers to the gate into the city of Jerusalem which at the time of this letter was looked upon as the camp of Israel. And just as the bodies of those animals that were sacrificed for sin were taken outside the camp of the Israelites, so Jesus made His sacrifice outside the camp of Israel. The blood He shed there is what sanctifies us or sets us apart.

1. 1 Cor. 1:2 - We are sanctified in Christ.
2. 1 Cor. 6:11 - We are sanctified in the name (power) of Jesus.
3. Eph. 5:26 - Jesus sanctified and cleansed us with the

washing of water by the word or by the new birth
(Jn. 3:3-5).

Verse 13: *Therefore let us go forth to Him, outside the camp,
bearing His reproach* - Just as Christ was sacrificed outside
the camp of the Jews they must go outside the sacrifices of the
Old Testament to the sacrifice of Christ. They must forsake
the camp of Israel, leaving Judaism as the means of justification and bearing the same reproach (rejection and ridicule)
that Jesus suffered.

1. 2 Tim. 3:12 - Paul said all Christians shall suffer
   pesecution.
2. Jn. 1:11-12 - Christ was rejected by the Jewish nation
   and these Hebrews would also be rejected for believing
   in Him.

Verse 14: *For here we have no continuing city, but we seek the
one to come* - I believe the city here to be the same city that
Abraham looked for that is mentioned in Hebrews 11:10 and
Hebrews 11:16. It is the city whose builder and maker is God.

Verse 15: *Therefore by Him let us continually offer the sacrifice of praise to God, that is, the fruit of our lips, giving thanks
to His name* – It is not by the sacrifices of the ceremonial laws
of Judaism but through the sacrifice of praise in giving to His
name that we honor God. The "sacrifice of praise" is here
identified as the "fruit of our lips giving thanks to His name,"
because out of the abundance of the heart the mouth speaks.
The sacrifice of praise and thanksgiving to God would express itself in all acts of adoration for God, which we can sacrifice acceptably to God *continually* through Christ.

1. 1 Pet. 2:5 - Christians are a holy *priesthood* and offer up
   spiritual *sacrifices* acceptable to God by Jesus Christ
2. Phil. 4:15-18 - Giving is a spiritual sacrifice of praise.

Verse 16: *But do not forget to do good and to share, for with such sacrifices God is well pleased* - We also sacrifice to God by doing good and sharing with others. These too are spiritual sacrifices we offer to God by Jesus Christ. The word "sacrifice" here is not to be taken in the sense of something that is offered as sacrifice for sin, or in the sense that we are doing good to attempt to make atonement for our transgressions, but in the sense of an *offering* made to God.

1. Eph. 4:28 - We are to work to give to those in need.
2. Gal. 6:10 - We are to do good as we have ability and opportunity.

Verse 17: *Obey those who rule over you, and be submissive, for they watch out for your souls, as those who must give account. Let them do so with joy and not with grief, for that would be unprofitable for you* - This refers to the Elders in the local church. We are to obey and submit to them in the matters that they have the authority to rule over. The early church had Elders who were to watch for the souls of those under their care. Generally they do the most work, yet receive the least pay and have more responsibility than anyone in the church. If we think about their work and responsibility, we shouldn't have any trouble submitting to them, whether we absolutely agree with their judgments or not.

Verse 18: *Pray for us; for we are confident that we have a good conscience, in all things desiring to live honorably* - This is a typical request of Paul and simply adds to evidence that he is the author (1 Thess. 5:25; Eph. 6:18, 19; 2 Thess. 3:2; Col. 4:3; Rom. 15:30; 2 Cor. 1:11). But be that as it may, the writer had a clear conscience and desired to live honorably in the world.

Verse 19: *But I especially urge you to do this, that I may be restored to you the sooner* - The writer is urging them to pray for him that he may be restored to them sooner. This statement is viewed by some as evidence that Paul was not the author of the book. They believe he was more associated with the church at Antioch than by the Jerusalem church, and they may be right. but is also true that he was well thought of and even considered part of the Jerusalem Church at one time (Acts 9:26-28).

1. Rom. 10:1-3 - Paul did care a lot about the Jewish nation.
2. Acts 11:29-30 - He and Barnabas brought some financial relief to Jerusalem.
3. Acts 24:10-17 - He did visit Jerusalem and even brought support to them.

Verse 20: *Now may the God of peace* - God is a God of peace.

1. 1 Cor. 14:33 - God is not a God of confusion but of peace.
2. Rom. 15:33 - He is referred to as a God of peace many times in the writings of Paul (Rom. 15:33; 16:20; 2 Cor. 13:11; Phil 4:9; 1 Thess 5:23).
3. Isa. 9:6-7 - Jesus is the Prince of peace.
4. Rom. 10:15 - The gospel is the gospel of peace.
5. Rom. 14:17 - The kingdom is a kingdom of peace.

who brought up our Lord Jesus from the dead - The resurrection of Jesus is of first importance (1 Cor. 15:1-4).

that great Shepherd of the sheep - He had mentioned the elders in verses 7 and 16 of this chapter and they are also "shepherds" of the sheep, but Jesus is the great Shepherd.

1. Jn. 10:11 - Jesus is the good Shepherd.
2. Heb. 13:20 - Jesus is the great Shepherd.
3. 1 Peter 5:4 - Jesus is the Chief Shepherd.
4. Ps. 23 - This chapter describes the Shepherd's care for His sheep.

through the blood of the everlasting covenant - Jesus is the great Shepherd of the sheep because He laid down His life for them. His blood is the everlasting covenant that God made with His people.

1. Heb. 8:13 - The Old Covenant was about to vanish away.
2. Lk. 22:20 - The sacrifice of Jesus is the New Covenant `God has made with man.
3. Heb. 13:20 - It is called the everlasting covenant because, unlike the Old Covenant, it is to last forever.

Verse 21: *make you complete in every good work to do His will, working in you what is well pleasing in His sight, through Jesus Christ, to whom be glory forever and ever. Amen* - The writer is here praying that God would fully endow them with whatever grace was necessary to do His will. He is working in every believer what is well pleasing in His sight through the power of the Lord Jesus Christ.

1. Phil. 2:12-13 – God works in us to do His will.
2. Eph. 2:10 - We are *His* workmanship.
3. John 15:5 - Without Him we can do nothing.
4. Rom.8:14 - We are led by His Spirit.

Verse 22: *And I appeal to you, brethren, bear with the word of exhortation,* - This letter was intended to be a word of encouragement to them.

for I have written to you in few words - This refers to the entire letter and it is short considering the subjects with which he deals. He could have written an entire volume of books if he had gone into detail on every subject he mentioned.

Verse 23: *Know that our brother Timothy has been set free, with whom I shall see you if he comes shortly* - The writer was evidently a close companion to Timothy. Some of us see this as more circumstantial evidence that Paul was the author. Timothy is represented as his constant companion and spoken of as a brother on more than one occasion (2 Cor. 1:1; Phil. 1:1; Col. 1:1).

Verse 24: *Greet all those who rule over you, and all the saints -* This greeting is sent to the Elders of the church as well as all of the members.

Those from Italy greet you - This was probably written from Italy perhaps when the writer was a prisoner there.

1. Hebrews 10:34 - The writer was in bonds when he wrote and was in Italy.
2. Acts 28:16, 17, 30, 31 - Paul was in chains in Rome, Italy.
3. It really does not matter in the least who wrote the book since we believe it is ultimately the Holy Spirit who inspired the words that were written regardless of the author. This is one reason that I have devoted very little time and space writing about it.

Verse 25: *Grace be with you all. Amen -* This is a great way to close the book. Regardless of the faults, failings, sins, and shortcomings these believers were dealing with, the Holy Spirit extends this blessing to all. *"Grace, grace, God's grace, grace that is greater than all our sins."*

Special Note: *Better News for the Hebrews* begins with Jesus (Heb. 1:1-3) and ends with Jesus (Heb. 13:20-21). How fitting since He is "the author and finisher of our faith" (Heb. 12:2). The better news is actually *great* news. The "great High Priest" (Heb. 4:14) who has provided us with "so great a salvation" (Heb. 2:3) is now the "great Shepherd of the sheep" (Heb. 13:20). This is a *great* way to close the Book of Hebrews as well as my book. Regardless of the faults, failings, sins, and shortcomings that all believers struggle with on a daily basis, the Holy Spirit appropriately ends His book as I do this one: "Grace be with you all. Amen."

Wayne Dunaway
November, 2017

Appendix # 1
"The World to Come"

The "world to come" is not here yet and no one is there yet. In my judgment the "world to come" is the "new heaven and new earth" that God promised to create for the saints in the Old Testament as well as the saints in the New (Isa. 65:17; 2 Pet. 3:13; Rev. 21:1). Many of us believe that there is something better awaiting the disembodied spirits of saints who die other than departing to be with Jesus at death. We believe that Jesus has something even better in store. Paul indicated that we desire to be clothed with our resurrection bodies and not be found naked, which indicates that we look forward to something *even better* than being a disembodied spirit in heaven (2 Cor. 5:1-4). The thing that will be better is that the disembodied spirits will be given resurrected bodies to live in eternally in the new heaven and new earth that God will create when the present one perishes.

I believe after the judgment we will be told by Jesus: *"Come you blessed of my Father inherit the kingdom prepared for you from the foundation of the world"* (Matt. 25:34). I believe that the Bible teaches that at death the "spirit" of the believer goes to heaven. For example, I believe that, like Elijah in 2 Kings 2:11, our spirits go directly to heaven when we die into the realm of the dead (hades) which is somewhere in heaven where Christ is (Phil. 1:21-23). I believe that our spirits remain there with Jesus until His second coming, at which time Jesus will bring disembodied spirits with Him to be reunited with our resurrected bodies and then we will be at the judgment, not to be judged but to be welcomed and rewarded (1 Thess. 4:14). It is then that we will receive the blessing that God has always had in mind for us—which is life in "a new heavens and new earth" (2 Pet. 3:13). It is my understanding that we do not go into the "new heavens and new earth" until after we are in our resurrected immortal bodies (1 Cor. 15:35) and after the judgment (Rev. 20:11-22:5). It is then that we enter the "world to come." The "world to come" is the world we enter after this world is destroyed (2 Peter 3:7-13). It is referred to in both Testaments as the "new heavens and the new earth" (Isa. 65:17; 2 Pet. 3:13; Rev. 21-22). It is the kingdom that we will "inherit" (not re-inherit) after the judgment (Matt. 25:34). It is the "everlasting kingdom" of our Lord Jesus Christ into which an entrance will be supplied to us abundantly when the "day of the Lord" comes (2 Pet. 1:11; 3:10). This is the *world to come* where all things will be in subjection to man as God intended in the beginning. The saints of all ages will reign/serve (Heb. 2:5-8) in the new heavens and new earth with God and the Lamb (Rev. 22:3-5). It is the "age to come" in contrast to "now in this time"—referring to time on this earth (Mk. 10:30). It is only fitting that God would refer to the *world to come* as a "new earth" because God created the present earth as the dwelling place for Himself and man in the beginning (Gen. 1-2). The glorified heaven and earth that God will create is referred to time and again in the Old Testament and promised to all of the faithful both then and now (Isa. 65:17; 2 Peter 3:13; Rev. 21-22:5). This is the earth that God was referring to when He said, *"the meek shall inherit the earth"* (Ps. 37:9, 11, 22, 29, 34; Matt. 5:5). God has promised all saints of all ages that this inheritance shall be forever (Ps. 37:18). The promise God made to Abraham and his seed is that he, as well as his descendants, would be the "heir of the world" (Rom. 4:13). The *world* that they are heirs of and joint-heirs with Christ is the world to come. But again the *world to come* is not here yet and none are there yet. As Peter said, *Nevertheless we, according to His promise, look for a new heavens and a new earth in which righteousness dwells* (2 Peter 3:13). This inheritance which is in the new heaven and new earth will likely be "in heaven" (1 Pet. 1:4) in the "Father's house" (Jn. 14:1-3). Some believe that it will be here on a renewed creation and that of course is possible. They base their view partly on the fact that John saw the bride, the Lamb's wife, coming down *out of heaven* from God to dwell in the *new heaven and new earth* that John saw after the first heaven and the first earth had passed away (Rev. 21:1-9). The exact location is not that important because whether here or there it will be great. As long as we know that the Holy Spirit referred to it as new heavens and a new earth in both Testaments that is the main thing that we are to look for (2 Pet. 3:13). John saw the New Jerusalem or bride of Christ coming down "out of heaven" from God to dwell forever and ever in the new heaven and new earth after the first heaven and first earth passes away (Rev. 21:1-3). This is the reason that my ultimate hope is living in the "new heaven and new earth" where the "tabernacle of God is with men" eternally much like in the Garden of Eden in the beginning but only much, much better (1 Cor. 2:9-10). It will be the time of "restoration" of all things after the present earth and heavens have passed away (Acts 3:21).

Appendix #2
"The Security of the Believer"

QUESTION: A good student of the Bible writes: "My question of the day is something I've been studying on and I wanted to know your thoughts on it. I've believed all my life that once I get sincerely born again and know it for sure, that I could never lose my salvation by disqualifying myself by slipping up and sinning. Everyone sins every day, right? What if I was born again and sinned for whatever reason and had no time to repent of it or ask forgiveness, and a truck hit me and I died. Would I go to hell because I didn't have enough time to ask forgiveness? Is once saved always saved true?"

MY ANSWER: I, too, believe in the security of the believer. A believer is one who trusts in, and relies on, the sacrifice of Jesus to save him and his faith shows itself in seeking to follow the Lord and do His will (Jam. 2:17-18). I believe that all believers do sin (1 Jn. 1:8), but the blood of Jesus keeps us cleansed from our sins (1 Jn 1:7). I do not believe that God counts the sins of a believer against him, because they are continually forgiven by the sacrifice of Jesus (2 Cor. 5:18-19). Therefore, if a believer "sinned and had no time to repent of it and ask for forgiveness and a truck hit him and he died," I do __not__ believe that he will be lost because God does not impute or count the sins to a believer against him/her (Rom. 4:8; 2 Cor. 5:17-19).

I believe that once a sinner becomes a believer (born again, Jn. 3:3-5) that he/she is always in a saved state as long as he <u>continues to believe</u>. In 1 John 5:13 the Bible says:

> *∗These things I have written to you who believe in the name of the Son of God, that you may know that you have eternal life, and that you may continue to believe in the name of the Son of God* (NKJV).

* In Revelation 2:10, Jesus said, *"Be faithful* (continue to trust in Jesus) *until death and I will give you the crown of life."* Why tell them to be faithful if being faithful is not necessary? If they were going to get the crown of life anyway, why did He say be faithful until death?

Another question we need to consider is: "Can a believer (one who trusts in Jesus) become an "unbeliever" (one who quits trusting in the sacrifice of Jesus)? Can a person who is "faithful" become "unfaithful?"

There are plenty of verses in the Bible that clearly say that a believer can become an unbeliever. A person who is a believer and who knows it for sure can quit trusting (believing) in Jesus, turn his back on Jesus, go back into the world of rebellion and sin, fall from grace, and be lost eternally.

Note the following verses from the letter to the Hebrew believers:

* *Wherefore, <u>holy brethren, partakers of the heavenly calling</u>, consider the Apostle and High Priest of our profession, Christ Jesus;* (Hebrews 3:1).

Observe that these were holy brethren and partakers of the heavenly calling. Then observe also what the writer said to these saved people:

* *Take heed, <u>brethren</u>, lest there be in any of <u>you</u> an evil heart of <u>unbelief</u>, in <u>departing from</u> the living God* (Hebrews 3:12).

Notice that these "holy brethren" who were "partakers of the heavenly calling" were warned that any of you could have "an evil heart of unbelief" and depart from God.

Note also that in the churches of Galatia some had "become estranged" or alienated from Christ. These had stopped trusting in His sacrifice and started trusting in their law keeping to save them:

> * *You have become estranged from Christ, you who attempt to be justified by law; you have fallen away from grace.* (NKJV). The NIV has: *You who are trying to be justified by law have been alienated from Christ; you have fallen away from grace* (Gal. 5:4).

Observe that he did not say, imply, or insinuate that they could not fall from grace, but rather he said *"you have fallen away from grace."* It is also interesting that the only time the Bible specifically mentions *"falling from grace"* it was because some had fallen from grace (Galatians 5:4).

Therefore, it seems to me that the Bible clearly teaches that it is possible for a Christian to turn away from Christ and be lost eternally because of it.

However, I do not believe that one can, or will, "lose his salvation by slipping up and sinning" as long as he does not lose his faith in Jesus. But it is possible and it has happened that Christians renounce their faith and quit trusting in Him at all. They now have no faith in Him as is evidenced by the fact that they have quit the church altogether and live lives just like those in the world that do not and never have trusted in Him.

I am well aware of the numerous passages that teach that the believer is secure in Christ (Ps. 37:23-24; Jn 5:24 & 10:27-30; Rom. 8:38-39; Heb. 13:5; Jude 1:1, etc.). I believe these verses are true and that the believer (one who continually trusts in Christ) is secure. However, I do not believe in the security of the unbeliever or one who has never trusted or one who ceases to trust in Christ.

Almost every book of the New Testament teaches that a believer must continue to believe in Jesus, or else, he will be lost. For example, read the following verses:

1. Matthew 25:14-30 - One of *His servants* was lost.
2. Mark 13:13 - He who *endures to end* will be saved.
3. Luke 8:13 - Some believe for a while, then *fall away*.
4. Luke 15:11-31 - A *son* was lost and is found.
5. John 15:1-5 - One who does not *abide* (continue/ remain) *in Him* is cast into fire.
6. Acts 1:25 - Judas by transgression *fell*.
7. Acts 8:13-24 - Simon (a *believer*) could perish if he did not repent.
8. Romans 8:13 - Christians who live after flesh *die spiritually*.
9. 1 Corinthians 8:11 - A brother can *perish* for whom Christ died.
10. 1 Corinthians 10:12 - Saints must take heed lest they *fall*.
11. 2 Corinthians 6:1 - Saints can receive *grace in vain*.
12. Galatians 5:4 - Some had *fallen from grace*.
13. Ephesians 5:3-7 -Wrath will come on *sons* of disobedience.
14. Philippians 3:12-14 - Christians must keep *reaching & pressing*.
15. Colossians 1:22-23 - Saved only if we *continue* in the faith.
16. 1 Thessalonians 3:1-8 - We live if we *stand fast* in the Lord.
17. 2 Thessalonians 2:15 - Christians must *stand fast*.
18. 1 Timothy 1:19-20 - Some had their faith to *shipwreck*.
19. 2 Timothy 4:10 - Demas *forsook* Paul having loved this present world.
20. Titus 3:8 - Believers must be careful to *maintain* good works.
21. Philemon 1:5 - Why mention faith if he did not

have to *keep it.*

22. **Hebrews 6:4-6 & 10:26-29 - Some *fall away* and forsake.**
23. **James 5:19-20 - A brother who *errs from truth* must be saved from death.**
24. **1 Peter 4:1 - Christians must *commit* souls to Him by doing good.**
25. **2 Peter 1:10 - Christians must take heed lest we *fall.***
26. **2 Peter 2:20-22 - Saints can go *back into world* and be overcome by it.**
27. **1 John 5:16 - Christians can commit a *sin unto death.***
28. **2 John 1:9-11 - We must *abide* in the teaching of Christ.**
29. **3 John 1:4 - Christians must *walk* in truth.**
30. **Jude 1:5 - He saved them, then *destroyed* those who did not believe.**
31. **Revelation 3:5 - Our name can be *blotted out* of the book of life.**

These are just some of the many verses that state or imply that believers must continue to believe in order to continue to be believers.

I know some who say, "If you got it, you can't lose it, and if you lose it, you never had it." I personally see no comfort or security in this statement. If this statement is true, then it seems to me that one would have to wait and make sure he did not lose it to know whether or not he ever had it! However, the Hebrew Christians had it (Heb. 3:1), and were warned time and again that they could lose it if: they forsook Christ, crucified Him afresh, counted His blood that had sanctified Him an unholy thing and had an evil heart of unbelief (Heb. 2:1-3; 3:12-13; 6:1-6; 10:25-29; & 12:25).

Also, I have heard something like, "If one's faith fizzles before the finish, then it was flawed from the first." Neither do

I see any comfort or security in this statement. If this statement is true, then, it would seem to me, that one would have to wait until the finish to know if his faith was flawed or not. If it fizzles then it is flawed, and if it does not fizzle then it is not flawed. But we will have to wait until the finish to see if we really have fizzling faith or finishing faith.

And to answer your last question: "Is once saved always saved true?"

Yes! A believer is always saved as long as he is a believer. But when one ceases to believe, then he ceases to be a believer and he will be lost. I believe that God is "*able to keep you from stumbling*" (Jude v. 24) and I believe that He will. However, He only keeps those who want to be kept. Therefore, believers have the responsibility to "*keep yourselves in the love of God*" (Jude v. 21) by continuing to trust in Him for salvation. I hope this helps.

Appendix #3
"Forsaking the Assembly"

Hebrews 10:25 is one of the most often quoted verses in some New Testament Churches. It has been used, sometimes abused and quite often misused. In this study we are going to look closely at the verse and answer three questions.

I.   What is forsaking the assembly?
II. What is the day approaching?
III. Why is this sin so serious?

I.   What is Forsaking the Assembly?

1. One of the worst sins that a Christian can commit is "forsaking the assembling" of the saints as per Hebrews 10:25.

2. It is by far and away one of the most obvious, most obnoxious and most offensive sins against Jesus that a child of God can commit.

3. I know this because of what the entire book of Hebrews teaches about it and especially in Hebrews 10:26-31.

4. How do we know that this sin is a very, very, very serious matter? Because:

> a. It is a willful sin (v. 26a).
> b. It is a sin that negates the death of Jesus (v. 26b).
> c. It is a sin that brings fiery judgment (v. 27b).
> d. It is a sin that makes us God's adversaries (v.27c).
> e. It is a sin that demands more severe punishment than rejecting the Law of Moses (vs. 28-29a).
> f. It is a sin that causes one to trample the Son of God underfoot (v. 29b).

g. It is a sin that causes one to count the blood of the covenant a common or unholy thing" (v. 29c.).

h. It is a sin that insults the Spirit of grace (v. 29d).

i. It is a sin that brings the vengeance of God (v. 30a).

j. It is a sin that makes it a fearful thing to fall into the hands of God (v. 31).

5. But what is it? Surely we need to know if it puts us in this predicament. Surely God makes it clear if it is this serious.

6. So what does "forsake" mean? Webster says it means "to renounce or turn away from entirely." It means "to leave without intending to return."

7. Strong says the Greek word means to totally abandon or utterly forsake.

8. Vine's Expository Dictionary says the word means to leave behind, to abandon.

9. Therefore *forsake* obviously means to quit, abandon, renounce, repudiate, to give up entirely, or to walk out on.

10. It is the same word that Jesus used in Matthew 27:46 when He said, *"My God, My God, why have you forsaken Me?"*

11. It is the same word that Paul used 2 Timothy 4:10 when he wrote, *"For Demas has forsaken me, having loved this present world."*

12. Therefore, it is clear that to forsake does not mean miss a service or fail to attend a Bible class. It means to abandon, give up completely, quit entirely and to refuse to assemble together.

13. The NIV says let us not give up meeting together and that is exactly what it means.

14. When we understand what *forsaking* really means then we can better understand why it is such a serious sin with such serious consequences. It actu-

ally amounts to forsaking Jesus!

II.   What is the Day Approaching?

1.   The second thing we need to consider in studying this verse is, "What is the day approaching?"
2.   Some think the "day" is the day of the Lord's second coming. I personally do not believe that that is the day, because no one can see it approaching (Mk. 13:31-32).
3.   A number of others believe that the *day* is the day of the destruction of Jerusalem that occurred in 70 A.D. I personally do not believe that is the day because I am not at all sure that they could see that day approaching. I realize that many appeal to Matthew 24:1-34; Mark 13:3-30; and Luke 21:7-32 and say that Jesus gave signs to tell them when the temple would be destroyed, but I am not sure that the statement is true. The disciples did not ask for, nor were they given, signs (plural) to tell them exactly when Jerusalem would be destroyed. In fact, in Mark 13:4 they specifically ask for "the sign" (not signs) that would tell them when the destruction of the temple would occur. In answering the question that they had asked, Jesus gave them the *sign* which was "when you see Jerusalem surrounded by armies, then know that its desolation is near" (Lk. 21:20). They did know that it would occur during "that generation" (Matt. 24:34) and possibly in a "little while" (Heb. 10:37), but that does not prove that they could actually see the day approaching. The things that Jesus mentioned that some think were signs of Jerusalem's fall such as wars, commotions, earthquakes, famines etc. were things which "must come to pass first, but the end is not immediately" (Lk. 21:9). Therefore these were not signs that would tell them that the day was

approaching. Furthermore, when that day approached they were to *"flee to the mountains"* (Lk. 21:20-21) not assemble with the members.

4. In my judgment the only *day* that they could actually see approaching was the day of the assembling -which was the first day of the week. It is called the "Lord's Day" (Rev. 1:10) and it was the first day of the week, when the disciples at Troas came together or assembled for worship (Acts 20:7).

5. If Paul "stayed seven days" evidently waiting for the first day of the week in Troas (Acts 20:7) then surely the Hebrews could "see" it approaching every week.

6. Of course, I am not alone in believing that the day was the day of assembling or the first day of the week. For example:

   a. Hugo McCord wrote: *"What day of assembly not to be forsaken could Christians (in the first century and now) see approaching? The apostle Paul, though on a hurried journey 'from Philippi' to get to 'Jerusalem on the day of Pentecost'(Acts 20:6), 'tarried seven days' in Troas, apparently waiting for 'the first day of the week' when the Christians in Troas would not forsake their assembling 'to break bread' (Acts 20:6-7)...Consequently, devoted Christians today, without a specific command, look back to the example set in Troas in 57 A.D., and from Monday on, through each week, can see the first day, Sunday, approaching. In love and appreciation they never want to forsake that special assembly set for the day they could see approaching."* (www.christianarticles.org/Articles/McCord/ assemblies.htm; Pg. 2)

   b. C.R. Nichol wrote, *"You should not only assemble, as you see the day approaching, you should exhort others to assemble. The "day approaching". What day? Certainly the day on which they "assembled", which was the first day of the week."* (Nichol's Pocket Bible Encyclopedia, pg. 118).

7. Some object to this view by saying that, if this is the case, one would have to start "exhorting" on Monday and increase all the more as Sunday approached. In other words, there would have to be "daily exhorting." And, in the case of the Hebrews, that could very well have been the case. They were to "exhort one another daily" (Heb. 3:13).

8. However, if the day was the day of the destruction of Jerusalem then I suppose, if that is the way we reason (?) about the verse, then they should have exhorted more and more as the day approached. The first week they could meet once for one hour, the second week they could meet twice for two hours and if they kept this pace up "so much the more" as the day approached, by the time the day arrived they could be meeting all seven days and for no telling for how long!

9. Of course, all of this is likely not at all what the writer meant. The writer is simply telling them to exhort one another to continue to be faithful and do it all the more when needed and as they had opportunity. Even daily if necessary (Heb. 3:13).

10. Also, if the day approaching was the day when Jerusalem was destroyed, then after the "day" was over what were they to do? Quit meeting together?

III.   Why Is This Sin So Serious?

1.   Our final question to consider in this study is this, "Why is this particular sin so serious with such serious consequences?"

2.   The answer seems to be that forsaking the assembly was evidence or proof that one had given up faith in Christ and His sacrifice.

3.   It is no wonder then that the consequences were so serious. It is no wonder that those who were guilty were in such a hopeless condition.

4.   When we consider the rest of the book of Hebrews we can easily see that the *forsaking* was a symptom of a heart problem—a heart that had renounced, rejected and repudiated the sacrifice of the Lord Jesus.

5.   For example, forsaking the assembling was the same as:

   a.   To "drift away" (Heb. 2:1).

   b.   To "neglect so great a salvation" (Heb. 2:3).

   c.   To have "an evil heart of unbelief" (Heb. 3:12a).

   d.   To be guilty of "departing from the living God" (Heb. 3:12b).

   e.   To be "hardened through the deceitfulness of sin" (Heb. 3:13).

   f.   To "fall away" (Heb. 6:6a).

   g.   To "crucify again for themselves the Son of God" (Heb. 6:6b).

   h.   To "put Him to an open shame" (Heb. 6:6c).

   i.   To "cast away your confidence" (Heb. 10:35).

   j.   To "draw back to perdition" (Heb. 10:39) or "turn their backs on God and seal their fate" (NLT).

   k.   To "turn away from Him who speaks from heaven" (Heb.12:25).

6.   When we look at the context of Hebrews, and what *forsaking the assembling of ourselves together* actually indicates, then we can easily see

that those guilty do indeed sin willfully; reject the only sacrifice for sins; have a fearful expectation of judgment and fiery indignation; become the Lord's adversaries; deserve a worse punishment than those who rejected Moses' law; and can expect vengeance from God (Heb. 10:26-29).

7. But to use this verse to condemn those who miss a worship service or a Bible class is, in my judgment, to misunderstand the meaning of the verse and misapply what it actually teaches.

www.ingramcontent.com/pod-product-compliance
Lightning Source LLC
Chambersburg PA
CBHW071524040426
42452CB00008B/874